The Civil War
in Hereford

The Civil War in Hereford

by

Ron Shoesmith

Logaston Press 1995

LOGASTON PRESS
Little Logaston Woonton Almeley
Herefordshire HR3 6QH

First published by Logaston Press 1995

ISBN 1 873827 34 2

Set in Baskerville 10/13pt and Lucida 9/13pt
by Logaston Press and printed in Great Britain
by Hillman Printers (Frome) Ltd

For Ruth

Contents

ACKNOWLEDGEMENTS

This book would not have been written without the help and encourage-
ment of City Councillor and past Mayor of Hereford, John Newman. He
not only took an interest in the subject, but also carried out much
research. John Newman, as much as anyone in the city, has taken the time
and made the effort to remind the citizens of Hereford of their proud
heritage. I hope that this book makes a small contribution towards encour-
aging and helping him in that aim.

The quotations used in this book are taken from a variety of 19th and early
20th century works listed in the Bibliography. There was no opportunity to
go back to the original sources, which are deposited in various Record
Offices across the country, but checks have been made where possible.

I am grateful to Ken Hoverd who copied many of the older photographs
used in this book and provided the present-day pictures. The drawings and
maps once again demonstrate the flair that Brian Byron brings to this type
of subject—he has my admiration and thanks. Jamesone's painting of
Alexander Leslie, Earl of Leven, is reproduced by courtesy of the Scottish
National Portrait Gallery; the paintings of John Speede by an unknown
artist, Sir William Waller also by an unknown artist, Charles I by Daniel
Mytens and Prince Rupert, Count Palatine, by Gerard Honthorst are
reproduced by courtesy of the National Portrait Gallery, London; and the
drawing entitled Interior of the Chapter House, Hereford Cathedral, by
William Stukeley (from MS. Top. gen. d. 13, fol. 24v) is reproduced by
courtesy of the Bodleian Library, Oxford. Thanks are also due to Hereford
City Council for permission to reproduce the city's coat of arms.

Great efforts were made to ensure that this book would be ready in 1995
for the 350 year celebration of the siege of Hereford—the efforts put in by

Andy Johnson of Logaston Press, who has published two of my previous books, are much appreciated. My thanks to John Eisel, who provided the information about All Saints Church, and Pat Hughes, for information about Joyce Jefferies house and the billeting of troops.

The final completion of any book is a time-consuming and worrying period. The worries inevitably carry over into my family life as the deadline approaches. My apologies to my wife, Ruth, and our children, Ben and Katy, for my shortcomings during that period and my thanks to them for their kindness and understanding.

INTRODUCTION

The Civil War in England during the middle years of the 17th century caused an immense amount of damage and destruction to property, set families against each other, and resulted in the execution of Charles I and the creation of a republic for a period of some ten years. The battles raged over the whole of the country and no individual was safe from bands of troops who systematically plundered their way through the English countryside.

There have been many books written about the Civil War, for, although it took place three hundred and fifty years ago, it is sufficiently recent for many written sources to have survived, either as published pamphlets and broadsheets or as correspondence and account books. In addition, petitions were sent to the two Houses of Parliament and reports of their deliberations have been kept. This material has, for many years, provided a fascinating source of study for historians and others with an interest in this period.

However, natives of Hereford reading most books about the Civil War would imagine that their city and county escaped virtually unscathed during this four year period of strife and bloodshed, for events in the city and county are written off in a few lines as being incidental to the main flow of the War.

This interpretation can be countered by the fact that Charles I granted the city an augmentation to its coat of arms including the motto 'Invictæ fidelitatis præmium'—'the reward for faithfulness unconquered', following a five week siege by the Scots army. In advance of this siege practically all the houses and other buildings in the suburbs outside the city walls and gates were deliberately dismantled or destroyed to allow the defenders clear lines of fire. During the siege the whole county suffered from the depredations of the invading army, many parishes being systematically plundered.

It is now over a hundred years since the Rev. John Webb wrote his *Memorials of the Civil War between King Charles I and the Parliament of England as it affected Herefordshire and the Adjacent Counties*. This two volume work, which was eventually edited and completed by his son, Rev. T.W. Webb, is the only detailed appreciation of the war in Herefordshire. It includes an especially useful appendix of documents of the period. John Webb and his son also produced the *Military Memoir of Colonel John Birch ... written by Roe, his Secretary, with an Historical and Critical Commentary*, which adds substantially to the latter part of the war. John Webb was a competent historian, a Fellow of the Society of Antiquaries, who gave two papers to the Society on *Some passages in the Life and Character of a Lady resident in Herefordshire and Worcestershire during the Civil War ... collected from her Account Book*. Without his research and dedication, the story of the city and county of Hereford during this fascinating period of the history of England, would be even less well known than it is now.

This book is the story of the city of Hereford and its citizens throughout the period of the Civil War. It is the story as it was told then, using contemporary documents wherever they are available, written by the people who were involved. Almost without exception, the people of Herefordshire supported the Royalist cause and the balance of documentary evidence reflects this. However, there is material relating to Parliament's supporters and this often provides conflicting evidence. It is for you, the reader, to make the final interpretations as the three hundred and fiftieth anniversary of the siege of Hereford arrives.

RON SHOESMITH
July 1995

CHAPTER ONE

Hereford—from its origins to the 17th century

The origins of a recognisable urban settlement at Hereford are obscure, for there is no documentary evidence and any archaeological evidence that may still survive remains buried and well hidden. The older part of the city is built on a gravel terrace overlooking the River Wye, close to its junction with the River Lugg. One likely route of the Roman road that followed the Welsh border, linking the two legionary fortresses of Chester and Caerleon, crossed the Wye at the ford after which Hereford is named. It is quite possible that, during an early period in the history of this border area, there was a ferry and a few associated buildings—more of a posting house or inn, rather than a settlement—next to the ford.

Following the Roman period, the origins of Hereford as a religious centre may be sought in a collegiate establishment which, for several hundred years before the Norman Conquest, occupied the area that was to become Hereford's castle. This religious settlement, eventually dedicated to St. Guthlac, could have been one of the ancient Welsh 'clas' churches, thus predating the foundation of the cathedral.

The Hereford diocese was formed from part of the massive Lichfield diocese about AD 676 with Putta as bishop, but there is no confirmation that his seat was at Hereford. Indeed, the earliest documentary evidence for a cathedral at Hereford is in AD 803 when Wulfheard describes himself as *Herefordensis Ecclesiæ Episcopus*. It has to be assumed that a small town grew around the cathedral, providing for the tradesmen and workmen that would have been needed for this remote foundation on the Welsh border—the only Saxon settlement west of the River Severn.

1

Around the middle of the 9th century the central 13 hectares of the growing city, which included a laid-out grid pattern of streets, was enclosed with a gravel embankment and ditch. Following a renewal of Danish raids, the defences were completely rebuilt and extended to the east to include the St. Guthlac precinct, possibly by Alfred (871-901). The timber face of that defence would not have lasted long and it was replaced in stone, probably during the reign of Edward the Elder (901-25) or Athelstan (925-40). The city was sacked by the Welsh in 1055 and refortified by Harold Godwinson the following year.

Immediately after the Norman Conquest, William fitzOsbern, a close friend of the Conqueror, was made Earl of Hereford. FitzOsbern was responsible for the safety of the vulnerable western border of England from Chepstow in the south as far north as Ludlow. He must have seen Hereford as the central point in his defensive system and made immediate efforts to increase the size and importance of the castle at the expense of the monks at St. Guthlac's.

One of William the Conqueror's most important achievements was his policy of conciliation with the Welsh princes. This meant that Hereford could expand safely outside its old Saxon defences without fear of attack from its western neighbours. FitzOsbern conceived a grand scheme which was to affect the city's design and development to the present day. In essence, he created a new town to the north of the Saxon city to be colonised by settlers, tempted to move from Normandy to Hereford by tax incentives.

The Saxon town had only two wide streets—Broad Street, running northwards from the ford across the river to a north gate in front of All Saints Church, and King Street, which then ran to the north of the cathedral to join into Castle Street. The narrow north-south streets that made up the grid pattern—Berrington Street, Aubrey Street, Church Street, St. John Street, Ferrers Street and St. Ethelbert Street—still remain.

The focus of fitzOsbern's new town was a vast market-place laid out to the north of the Saxon defences and based on the lay-out of one he knew well at Breteuil in Normandy. The new market place comprised the triangle of land now bounded by Commercial Street, Union Street and St. Peter's Street. It was approached by new, wide roads—St. Owen's Street from the south-east, Commercial Road from the north-east, and Eign Gate Street and Bewell Street combined together to make the grand entry from the west. Indeed, the present High Town was merely part of this grand western approach, linked to the narrow Widemarsh Street, the old Saxon road leading towards the ford across the Wye. Surrounding this vast, open space were the long, narrow burgage plots of the Norman settlers. The scheme was successful—the Domesday Survey of 1086 indicates that by that date there were people living inside and outside the old defences. By then Hereford had a mint and there were seven moneyers.

The market-place would originally have contained flimsy stalls, but, as the traders became more successful, the stalls would have become more permanent structures and eventually they would have had living accommodation built above them creating upper floors. The main triangle is now full of buildings, as indeed was High Town until the clearance that took place at the beginning of the 19th century.

The original Saxon population of Hereford was left more or less alone in the old town, but with two significant changes—the cathedral precinct was increased across the old west-east street to make space for a new, vast cathedral, and the eastern part of the city was taken over for the new castle. The only convenient means of access from the old town into the new market was the old Saxon gate at the northern end of Broad Street. Gradually, informal passages were created across the old defensive line—a path over the embankment and possibly a plank bridge across the wet moat. After some nine hundred years some of these ways still survive in the northern part of Church Street, the Booth Hall passage, Barroll Street, and the recently-widened Offa Street.

FitzOsbern was killed in 1071 and shortly afterwards his son Roger was involved in an unsuccessful attempt to depose the king. This meant that the castle became a Royal possession and other Norman lords started to take an interest in the city. One of these was Walter de Lacy who made significant alterations to the approach roads leading to the market. These roads were so wide that there was room for substantial buildings in the middle and de Lacy took advantage of this to build St. Owen's Church at the eastern limit of the new city in St. Owen's Street. Similarly All Saints Church was built in the western approach road, directly outside the old gateway that led into the Saxon town. Was a third church planned for Commercial Road (earlier Bye Street) but never built? There may have been a change of mind, for, during the latter part of the 11th century, de Lacy was also responsible for building St. Peter's monastery and church in the southern part of the market-place. This was his final work in Hereford—when inspecting the new building in 1095, he died as a result of a fall from the battlements.

Hereford Castle was one of the earliest in England, being built by Ralph, the son of the Count of Vexin, before 1052. It was probably small, of motte and bailey design, occupying the eastern corner of the defended

John Speede's map of Hereford in 1610

Saxon city, close to the east gate. Hoggs Mount, the high point at the north-eastern corner of Castle Green, may represent this castle. William fitzOsbern was responsible for the immediate post-Conquest growth of the castle and may have built the vast new mound or motte that stood to the west of Castle Green in the area now called Redcliffe Gardens. Throughout most of its active life the castle was a royal stronghold and, because of its position near the Welsh border, had an almost constant building programme that made it one of the strongest castles in the land. The great keep or 'dungeon' (after the French, *donjon*) on top of the mound, consisted of a great tower surrounded with a wall that included ten semi-circular towers. The bailey of the castle—the area now known as Castle Green—was full of buildings including halls fit for the king and queen and their retinue whenever they visited the city, stables, gaols, kitchens and even a building in which siege engines were kept.

John Speede, by an unknown artist

The Edwardian conquest of Wales between 1277 and 1282 meant that Hereford lost much of its strategic importance. The castle was allowed to fall into a ruinous state and, although it was repaired in the early 15th century at the time of the Glyndwr uprising, it 'tendithe toward ruine' when Leland visited a hundred years later. There is no record of any work being carried out between the early 15th century and the time of the Civil

War, so substantial repairs would have been necessary to make it defensible.

The first city charter, granted by Richard I in 1189, allowed the citizens to fortify their city. Initially, they built a new earthwork defence that enclosed the 38 hectares of both old and new towns. By 1265 a stone wall had been added to the embankment for the whole of the 1,265 metre circuit. It included sixteen semi-circular towers and six gates and was surrounded by a water-filled ditch. The only gateway of the old Saxon city to be reused was at the western end of the old main street. Friars Gate, as it was eventually called, had relatively little use, for the main western gate, Eign Gate, was the one that led into the Norman town. Widemarsh Gate controlled traffic coming into the city from the north, whilst Byster's or Bye Street Gate faced the north-east towards Bromyard and Worcester. The road from St. Owen's Gate, on the south-east of the city, led towards the bridge across the River Lugg at Mordiford and thence to Ross and Gloucester. The sixth gate was on the southern end of the bridge that by then had been built across the Wye. The present bridge replaced this early structure in 1490. The walls and gates were apparently kept in a reasonable state of repair until the 17th century.

The cathedral church of the Virgin Mary and St. Ethelbert stands in the middle of the Saxon city. The present building was started by bishop Robert of Lorraine (1079-1096) and the main work was completed by 1148. In 1234 the east end was remodelled by the addition of the Early English Lady Chapel and the north transept was built (or rebuilt) in the 1260s. The central tower, which once supported a spire, has a wealth of ball-flower ornamentation. Until the collapse on Easter Monday, 1786, the cathedral had an equally high west tower.

Between the cathedral and the river are the Bishop's Palace, which incorporates parts of the 12th century great hall built by bishop William de Vere, and the College of the Vicar's Choral, which was built between 1472 and 1475. The latter contained 27 two-roomed houses, a hall and a chapel, all set out around a quadrangle. The college is joined to the cathedral by an open cloister and to the west of this and south of the south transept was the decagonal chapter house.

Besides All Saints and St. Peter's, the two churches in fitzOsbern's market-place, there were three other churches associated with the medieval city: St. Nicholas, at the junction of Bridge Street and King Street near the middle of the Saxon town; St. Owen's, just outside the defences to the east of the walled city; and St. Martin's, in the bridgehead settlement that gradually grew on the southern bank of the Wye.

The pre-Conquest collegiate establishment built close to the river and dedicated to St. Guthlac moved from its old location to a new site outside Bye Street Gate in 1144. This followed the 'trouble and strife' that occurred during the battles associated with the weak reign of Stephen and the attempts of Matilda's supporters to gain her the throne. The Franciscans (Greyfriars) had a house outside the defences to the west of the city and the Dominicans (Blackfriars) had their precinct on the eastern side of Widemarsh Street a little way outside the gate.

This was the walled city visited by John Leland, just over a hundred years before the events recorded in this book. Very few people had travelled through England and Wales before the Civil War—John Leland was an exception. He was born at the beginning of the 16th century and educated at Cambridge, Oxford and Paris. In 1533 he received a commission to search monastic and collegiate libraries for forgotten 'monuments of ancient writers.' These, his first journeys, took place before and during the Dissolution—a time when he gained an appreciation of the topography of the country and brought books and library lists back to London. At a later date he went on extended antiquarian and topographical tours during which he made notes in diary form. These notes, which now comprise the well-known *Itinerary*, were never intended to be published in that form, but by the age of forty his mind had failed, and he died in 1552.

His notes provide the first detailed description of the country as a whole and give a vivid impression of the difficulties of travel in the 16th century and the state of the various towns he visited. They provide a picture of the city of Hereford and of the condition of the defences and the castle which altered little over the following hundred years.

Leland's first visit to Hereford was during one of his tours through England and Wales between 1536-39. He came from south Wales through Monmouth, and after visiting Hereford went on to Leominster and Ludlow:

> Cummynge from Monemuthe into Herford I passed over a large bridge of stone set on iiii arches. This town is auncient, large and strongely walled, also having a mayne castel hard by the ripe of Wy. I take the castel to be of as great circuite as Windesore. The dungyn of the castel is hy and stronge, and yn the dyke not far from yt is a fair spring cawlled S. Ethelbertes Well ... The walle of the towne is cumpased with a dike alway filled with morisch water gethering and descending onto hyt. Certen mylles servid with this water causeth the town dikes

alway to have water, els they wold often be dry. This water resorteth to the botom of Wy. There be in the towne iiii paroche chyrches (one of them is yn the cathedral chirche) wherof certeyne be very fair, beside the cathedral chirche, the which is of a very strong building ... Ther be in the suburbes ii paroche chirche[s], a celle of Blak Monkes longing to Glocester Abbay, ii houses of Freres Blak and Gray. Sum say that the town toke the name that yt hath now of an old forde or passage over Wy, not far from the castel.

Leland returned for a second visit to the city a few years later. He was then on his way from Gloucester to Shrewsbury and probably came up the eastern side of the Wye crossing the Lugg at Mordiford Bridge on his approach to Hereford. He must have spent some time in the city during this visit for his description is very comprehensive. It is given in the note form in which it was written.

The towne of Hereforde stondithe somewhat lowe on every syde. There be hills by est and southe on the ryght rype of Wy ryver, well wooddyd, and not far distaunt from Hereforde toune.

The name of Hereford toune of some in Welche is caulyd Heneford of an old forde by the castle, by the whiche many passyd over, or evar (before) the great bridge on Wy at Herford were made.

The towne selfe is within the compasse of the walls a good mile.

There be in the wauls of Hereford 6 gates: Wy Gate; Frere Gate standithe west, caullyd of the Grey Freres house standinge without it; Inne Gate toward west north west; Wigmarsh Gate flat northe; [Wigmarch a marsh ground a little without the gate or suburbe:] Bysshop Strete Gate northe est; St. Androws Gate by est, so caullyd of St. Androwes pariche in the suburbes without this gate.

There is a litle broke that cummithe a 5 miles by west from Hereforde, and so circuitithe the diches of Herford towne walls, *ubi non defenditur vaga*, and goithe downe levynge the castle on the right hand, and there drivynge 2 mills for corne goith into Wy a flite shot bynethe Wy bridge and hard by benethe the castle.

The waull and gates of Herford be right well maintainyd by the burgesses of the towne.

The castle of Hereford standithe on the southe syde of the towne hard apon Wy bynethe Herford bridge. It was a great thing.

There be 4 paroche churches within the waulls, St. Peter, St. Nicholas, Alhallows, and St. John's.

The cathedrall churche stondithe in the southe parte of the towne as in the highest grownd of it nere to the castle.

There is a suburbe without Wy-Gate, and therein is a chapell of our Lady of Alingtre *prope furcas*, another of S. Aegidii. There is a churche of St. Martin in Wy-Gate suburbe bynethe the bridge.

The brige ovar Wy hathe ... great arches of stone.

There be but few howses without Freres Gate.

There is a suburbe without Inne Gate, and in it is a chappell of St. Giles first founded for Lazars, now convertyd to the use of othar pore folke.

There is a suburbe without the north-gate alias Wigmarche Gate. [This] is the fayrest suburbe of the towne. In this suburbe was the Blake Friers, first foundyd by Deinville a knight and finished by Edward the third.

There was an hospitall of St. John, sometym a howse of Templaries, now it is an almeshouse with a chaple. At the northe ende of this suburbe is a broke callyd Smaul Purse, cumming out of a [medowe called] Brode Medow thereby. It rennithe by the Blake Freres, and drivynge mils goithe under Ine Bridge of one stone arche and so into Wy.

There is a praty suburbe without Bysshops-gate-Strete. There was the priory of St. Guthelake, a cell to Glocestar.

There is a suburbe without St. Andrew's gate. There is a parocshe church of St. Andrew in the midle of the strete. There is an hospitall of St. Giles, wher ons wer friers Graye and the Templaries. Kynge Richard gave this chapell to the towne, and then it was mad an hospitall.

During this visit he also spent some time around the castle, providing the only detailed description after it had fallen into disuse, but before it was demolished. Written towards the middle of the 16th century, the report can be compared with the illustration of the castle included in Speede's map of 1610.

The castle of Hereford stondithe on the lifte ripe of Wy ryver, and a litle benethe the bridge, and is strongly diched *ubi non defenditur flumine*. The waules of it be highe and stronge, and full of great towres, but now the hole castle tendithe toward ruine. It hath bene one of the fairest, largest and strongest castles of England. It hathe 2 wardes, and eche of them were environid with water. There cam an arme of a broke that rennithe thrwgh a great pece of the towne dike by an arche made in the towne waulle into the castle dyke, and so compassynge halfe the castle went into Wy: so that withe the principall arme of it goinge throughe the castle dike, and with the mayne streame of Wy river, the hole castle was environyd; but now the arme of the broke cumithe not thorwe the castle, yet might it be sone returnyd thither.

The second warde where the dungeon is was also environyd withe watar. For a pece of the watar that cam thrwghe the dyche was turnyd that way.

The dungeon of the castle is highe and very stronge, havynge the utter waull or warde 10 towres *forma semicirculari*, and one great towre in the inner warde.

There was one great bridge of stone archis, and a draw breidge in the midle of it, to entre into the castle. It stode on the northe west syde of it. It is now clene downe.

There is a faire chapell of St Cuthebert, the este parte whereof is made *opere circulari*. There were sometyme prebendaries; but one of the Laceis translatyd them thens onto St. Peter's in Hereford towne, and that coledge was thens translatyd into the este suburbe of Hereford, and a priorie of monkes erectyd there, and made a cell to Glocestar.

There is a fair and plentifull springe of water within the castell, and that and the pece of the broke comminge out of the diche dyd drive a mille within the castle.

After the Dissolution, the monastic settlements were sold off and parts of the buildings were converted to become houses. Sir Thomas Coningsby had built a house on the site of the Blackfriars priory, to the north of the city outside Widemarsh Gate, by 1613, and John ap Rice had bought St. Guthlac's priory and its precincts, outside Bye Street Gate, and had taken up residence there. In both cases the new owners made use of some parts of the existing buildings and either demolished the remainder or left

The Market Hall as depicted on Taylor's Map of 1757

them to become ruins. The buildings of the Greyfriars priory, a little way outside Friars Gate, were converted to housing, but were still recognisable when Speede drew his map of the city at the beginning of the 17th century.

Although there was a further outbreak of the plague in 1610 this does not seem to have had any great effect on the general prosperity of the city. Building work continued with the High Town market place gradually becoming filled with timber-framed buildings. Supreme amongst them was the Market Hall, some 85 feet long and 35 feet wide, supported on twenty-seven wooden pillars and standing three stories high with the ground floor left open for a market. It was built at the end of the 16th century and had rooms for the fourteen city guilds on the upper floor with the assize court and magistrates' chambers below them. Also in High Town, the Old House, once central to a row of buildings called The Butchery, is dated to 1621.

The well-established trade guilds, including bakers, barbers, butchers, clothiers, coopers, glovers, tanners and weavers, ensured that 'foreign' and presumably cheap competition was barred from the city. The general picture is of a county town with a well-patronised market and a good measure of civic pride. Indeed, much of this period, a few decades before the outbreak of the Civil War, could well have been one of the most affluent in the city's history.

Hereford as it would have appeared shortly before the Civil War
(Model in the Old House)

CHAPTER TWO

Build-up to the War

It is some three hundred and fifty years since this country was engulfed in the Civil War—a war in which Parliament opposed the Crown; a war that involved misery and death to thousands and set families against each other; a war that resulted in the execution of the king, Charles I, and the formation of a republic. Its roots lay in a number of grievances which even Parliament itself found difficult to define when an attempt was made shortly before the restoration of the monarchy and the coronation of Charles II.

The Long Parliament, so-called since it survived from its foundation in November, 1640, until it was dissolved on 16 March, 1660, started with a full complement of members. It was reduced to about 80 in 1648 following Pride's Purge of those considered to be antagonistic to the army, whilst the survivors, known as the Rump Parliament, were expelled by Cromwell in 1653 and did not meet again until after he had died in 1658. When they finally reassembled in December, 1659, they spent several days debating the causes of the war and could come to no definite conclusion. These days there tends to be a rather simplistic picture of Roundheads versus Cavaliers, Parliamentarians versus Royalists, and we see the war as one to decide who should rule the country—the people or the king. But the causes of the English Civil War were much more complex than this, and gradually accumulated during the early part of the reign of Charles I.

The son of James I of England (and James VI of Scotland), Charles was born in 1600. Apart from his general education, he must have been influenced to a considerable degree by his father who was a fervent Protestant, responsible for the publication of the Authorised Version of the Bible; a landmark for literature as well as religion. James was also the first king of both England and Scotland, and a ruler who constantly preached 'the divine right of kings'. Although he survived the Gunpowder Plot, that treasonable attempt brought about a new wave of anti-Catholicism and religious intolerance to the country which was to continue well into the reign of his son.

Charles came to the throne following the death of his father in 1625. Although without any doubt a courageous man of high principles, he was stubborn and appears to have lacked good judgment. This may have been partly because he was a poor communicator due to his stammer. This affliction also made him over-reliant on a clique of friends who were often more likely to do him harm than good and who kept him at a distance from government officers.

Even his marriage caused problems. His wife, Henrietta Maria, daughter of Henry IV of France, was a Catholic. She brought many of her Catholic friends to Court, causing much friction and bad feeling amongst the staunch English Protestants.

From the beginning of his reign Charles refused to accept the rule of Parliament, especially when a Bill of Rights was proposed. Although without proper authority, he continued to collect customs dues, then normally granted to the sovereign through Parliament. He also raised additional income by enforcing 'loans' from the gentry, with prison as a penalty for those who did not pay, and by the medieval system of 'fines' from those who had sufficient income but had not accepted knighthood with its consequential duties and costs. In 1629, he dissolved Parliament for a third time and began an eleven year period of direct personal rule. The Parliament he dissolved included as one of its more outspoken members the constitutional lawyer Sir Edward Coke. Coke had forever argued that 'the law' was greater than the king and that therefore 'the king cannot by proclamation create an offence which was not an offence before; that the king's proclamation forms no part of the law; and that he hath no prerogative but that which the law of the land allows him.' The seeds of division were already laid.

Initially Charles started his direct rule well. By making peace with France and Spain he saved expenditure and gradually restored his battered finances to some degree of health. However, he had little choice but to find new methods of raising money in as legal a form as possible. One such method, the cause of much resentment throughout the country, was a tax called Ship Money.

Although this tax had been in existence for many years as an aid to maritime defence, levying had been restricted to coastal ports. In 1635,

Charles I, by Daniel Mytens

Charles extended the tax to the whole kingdom, ostensibly to ensure that everyone had to pay towards the cost of defending the country, but actually to ensure that his total income was greatly increased. Initially successful in raising revenue, opposition grew as people came to appreciate that the king could raise it without obtaining the consent of Parliament and, well before it was abolished by the Long Parliament in July, 1641, it had become one of the major grievances the landed classes had against the king. The citizens of Herefordshire must have had somewhat ambivalent feelings about it, for whilst hardly any of them would have seen the sea, let alone the ships that sailed upon it, they were supporters of the crown. Charles tested this loyalty against the increasing financial burden they had to bear, a burden especially keenly felt by the growing commercial classes.

The responsibility for collecting the tax lay with the sheriffs. In Herefordshire in 1636 this was Roger Vaughan, who appears to have approached the task with some concern. He reported to the Privy Council:

> According to the commands of your Lordships' letters, dated the 9th of October, I have here inclosed sent your Lordships a true Certificate of the several sums set upon each parish in general within this county of Hereford, for the Shipping Money; the which, as I find it a heavy service, so I can do no less than inform your Lordships, that so great a sum in so small and so poor a shire cannot be raised but with much difficulty. Humbly beseeching your Lordships not to take it ill, that I do inform you, that I believe, for so small a circuit of ground as this shire contains, there are not in this kingdom a greater number of poor people, having no commodity amongst us for the raising of money, but some small quantities of fine wooles, which is now decayed for divers years past, by the importation and use (as is conceived) of Spanish wooles into this kingdom.

Included with this letter was a certificate itemising, parish by parish, the amounts set upon them 'for the furnishing of One Ship, of Three Hundred and Fifty Tons, for the Safeguard of the Seas, and Defence of the Realm.' This would ostensibly have been a 28 gun sloop manned by around 110 men.

A few examples from parishes close to Hereford gives an indication of the amounts expected:

16

Withington	£31 10s. 0d.
Mordiford & Dormington	£20 9s. 4d.
Holmer & Shelwick	£13 0s. 9d.
Hampton & Tupsley	£24 11s. 9d.
Lugwardine	£19 6s. 9d.

The city of Hereford was assessed at £220; Leominster at £44; and Ledbury at £61 7s. 4d. The total amount for the county for 1636 was £3,501 9s. 4d.

Complaints against the tax were increasing throughout the country and Hereford was very much in the forefront—the city's concerns were outlined in a Presentment by the Grand Jury in 1640. But by this date, towards the end of the period of Charles's personal rule, grievances were being aired on more than just the issue of Ship Money and several were included in the Presentment:

> Wee finde and present that the Weares erected in & upon the River of Wye within this County, being a Navigable Ryver, and not by the sea Coaste, are not prostrated and putt downe accordinge to the statute of Magna Charta, but are remayneing a greate Nusance and greevance to this County, soe farre as they hinder navigation and portacon of boates, and especially a prejudice to the Citty of Hereford, and are alsoe a distrucon of the ffry of fishe and a hurte to the Countrey in surrounding of grounds.
>
> Wee finde and present that the importacon and workinge of Spanish Wooll in this kingdom, comonly called sigovia or spanishe wooll, hath bynne, and still is a cause and meanes that the native wooll of this Countie of Hereford is made of less value and reputacon than otherwise it would bee to the greate damadge of the whole Countie.
>
> Item wee finde and present that the exercise of the Jurisdiccon of the Lord President and Councell, established for Wales and the Marches of the same, in the County of Hereford beinge an ancient Englishe County, and noe pte of Wales nor the Marches of the same, is and hath bynne a burden and grevance to this County, from wch the said Countie desire to be freed and eased.
>
> Item wee doe alsoe finde and present that the late taxacon upon this County for raiseinge of Money for buildinge and

Maintenance of shipps of warre for these five yeares last past hath bynne a great chardge greevance and Impoverishinge to the Comon Wealth of the same; from wch the said County desire to be freed; And also doe finde and present that the levyinge of the unlawfull taxe of Coate and Conduct money within this County hath likewyse bynne a great chardge and trouble to the whole County in generall, and is a gen'all greife and Nusance to the County.

We doe alsoe finde and present that the iron Mills in gen'all within this County have byne a gen'all distruccon of Trees, Tymber and Coppice wood some of which beinge within five Miles of the Cittie of Herf., in soe much that the said Cittie is already in greate want and scarcity of wood, and by reason thereof, the Prices of Wood is soe Inhaunced, that if it should Contynue, it would tend to the great impoverishinge of the Inhabitants of the said Citty and many places adjacent to the same.

Endorsed, Hereff. grievances

The mention of navigation on the River Wye is of some interest for it was not until after the Civil War that any real efforts were made to control the river. The first attempt was in 1662 when Sir William Sandys and several of his relatives obtained a private Act of Parliament empowering them to 'make navigable or passable by barges, boats, lighters and other vessels the rivers Wye and Lugg and the rivulets and brooks and other watercourses running into them in the Counties of Hereford, Gloucester and Monmouth.' The complaint may have been partly due to the fact that in 1527 the king had ordered that the four mills and weirs on the Wye at Hereford be demolished. However, the Dean and Chapter were given permission to rebuild them in 1555 and this Presentment may well have been another attempt to open the river to all traffic.

The extensive use of timber in the iron mills had been a growing problem in Herefordshire and the surrounding counties for many years. As wood was cut down or coppiced, the stocks were not replaced by new timber. This not only affected the citizens who wanted to heat their homes, it also created a shortage of raw material for building new houses. The problem was not properly resolved until a regular supply of coal became available from barge traffic on the Wye, and brick, baked in local fields, became the new building material.

As for the hated Ship Money, a challenge against the tax was mounted in the civil courts, but the judges decided that the levy was lawful.

North East View of the City of Hereford.

Hereford from Aylestone Hill (Probably copied from the Buck 1732 engraving). St. Owen's Gate is on the far left; the cathedral still has its spire and west tower; central is the tower of St. Nicholas Church; to the right are the spires of St. Peter's and All Saints. Bye Street suburb is on the far right

19

Opposition could have ended there had it not been that the fleet, provided from this tax, was used for several dubious causes. On one occasion Charles used it to transport Spanish gold to pay her troops who were then fighting Protestant Holland, and on another the fleet intervened on behalf of Spain to lift a French and Dutch siege of Dunkirk. Fears of a Catholic plot based around Charles's Catholic queen began to surface. These fears grew when Charles tried to bring over Catholic Irish troops to suppress a Scottish rebellion, a rebellion which arose over a mixture of religious and nationalistic grounds.

Although the Reformation had had over a hundred years to settle down, England was still in the throes of a religious fundamentalist revival that emphasised the importance of the individual and believed that man could be saved by his faith alone. The Puritans added to this general cult of the individual for they accepted a measure of predestination and considered that all men were equal in the eyes of God. They argued that by a study of the bible, hard work and practising a sober life, salvation was guaranteed.

Charles's religious policy was largely the work of William Laud, Bishop of London and later Archbishop of Canterbury. He was a believer in ritual and ceremony within the church and approved of vestments for the priest—the very things that the Puritans most despised, for they saw them as relics of the hated popery. In 1635, Laud gained the initiative and once again established the privileged position of the clergy by a simple change. He decreed that the communion table should be moved from its position in the nave to the eastern end of the chancel and that it should be railed in. The Communion Rail—that great separation between the congregation and the priesthood—upset all well-intentioned Puritans. Once the Civil War was under way, it is not surprising to find that the soldiers in the Parliamentarian army felt that they had every right to strip all popish symbols from parish churches.

Laud was also opposed to the Puritan lay-preachers who were outside the control of the bishops. Eventually, in an ill-conceived attempt at conformity, he attempted to impose the English Prayer Book on the Scots. The Scots, already feeling that the English Church had retained at least many of the outward signs of Catholicism, reacted by producing the Scottish National Covenant in 1638. It was signed by many in Scotland, pledging themselves not to accept any religious innovations. Charles, as head of the Church, refused to accept it and decided to settle the issue by the sword. However, his hastily raised army was no match for the equally hastily raised Scottish force that had the advantage of officers with many years experience of war in Holland and Germany. By the Treaty of Ripon the Scots were allowed to occupy Northumberland and Durham, and to receive a subsidy of £25,000 per month. Charles's finances were in no state to afford this and, in desperation, he recalled Parliament. This, the Short Parliament, was not a success—it only lasted three weeks before being dissolved by the king. But the problem did not go away and six months later the Long Parliament was assembled.

Many Members of Parliament realised that at last they had some leverage over Charles in his need for finance, and a period of hard negotiations began. It was complicated by the fact that Parliament did not trust the king and the king did not trust Parliament. Indeed, the people as a whole did not trust the king, or more particularly his advisers, Archbishop Laud and Thomas Wentworth, Earl of Strafford. The king had to succumb to the force of popular feeling and Strafford, the man who a few months earlier had tried to bring over the Irish troops, was arraigned for serious offences against the country and in May, 1641, was executed. This was not sufficient to satisfy a Parliament long kept out of government and it sought to use its powers to reduce those of the king. Under the careful and dogged leadership of John Pym, Acts were passed abolishing Ship Money and the Court of the Star Chamber—used oppressively by the king during his period of personal rule. Charles was forced to give assent to the Triennial Act guaranteeing a Parliament of at least 50 days' duration every three years even in the event of the king's failure to move the appropriate writs. It was never used, for it was not applicable to the present Parliament, and the subsequent regular one, the Cavalier Parliament of 1664, modified it, but its enactment focussed attention on the growing constitutional divisions.

Rumours once more abounded that Charles was prepared to use force to bring Parliament to heel; Pym reacted by skilfully using the London mobs as a counter threat. Then came news of a rebellion by Irish Catholics in Ulster. The Thirty Years War had not yet run its full course and the cause of Protestantism was not yet secure. There was an urgent need for an army to be sent to safeguard the Protestant colony in Ireland. But could the king be trusted with such an army? Might he not use it against Parliament? Parliament reacted by debating a Grand Remonstrance of all remaining grievances in the hope that Charles would accept it and an army could then be raised to succour Ulster. Charles dallied in Scotland allowing Pym to tighten his grip in London and the Remonstrance was passed with a majority of 11 votes. Charles returned to London to dine and cajole his parliamentary supporters whilst promising to consider the Remonstrance. As a result of Charles's actions, the Royalist bloc in the Lords deleted a clause from a Commons' bill that would have taken away the king's power to compel men to undertake military service outside their counties, except in the event of external invasion. The Commons countered this defeat with a militia bill designed to transfer the control of all the armed forces to a Lord General appointed by Parliament.

Events moved fast. Charles rejected the Remonstrance; by return the Commons forged ahead with the militia bill. Rumours circulated that Pym was preparing to impeach the queen; Charles reacted by having articles impeaching Pym, four other M.P.s and one peer, read out in the House of Lords. The Lords prevaricated but Charles refused to be delayed by technicalities in the procedures over which the Lords wanted to reassure themselves. He sent guards to the Commons to arrest the five M.P.s, but they were sent away empty-handed. The next day Charles went to the Commons in person to arrest the five, but 'the birds had flown' and Charles had to withdraw with the cries of 'Privilege! Privilege!' ringing in his ears. The Commons immediately and illegally appointed an experienced soldier to command the city militia whilst Charles withdrew to Hampton Court. The following day Pym and his friends re-appeared in triumph in the House of Commons.

Neither the king nor Parliament could call on a standing army with which to quell the other, so both sides had to make arrangements and seek support. Each county had an arsenal and a trained militia. By passing the militia bill, Parliament effectively tried to place these trained bands under its own control. This forced Charles to issue Commissions of Array which allowed his named commissioners to take command of the troops. Events were moving to a dangerous pitch.

Charles hoped that by delaying matters he could break Pym's power by picking away at his support, but the rifts were starting to go so deep that both sides gradually attracted a larger and larger following as people were forced to take a stand. Charles decided to look for increased support in the north, but was refused entry into Hull, where the arms from the northern campaign were stored, and went on to York. Parliament, meanwhile, started to act as if their will was the same as the king's will. It followed that the resulting local arguments over who actually controlled the militia could only lead to fighting and the first skirmish took place on 15 July between rival partisans in Manchester. Charles decided he had to raise the royal standard and so flush out into the open all those who would defy it, hoping that this might persuade waverers of the consequences and bring them to his cause. The only remaining question was where to unfurl his standard.

The formal start of the Civil War is reckoned to be 22 August, 1642, when Charles raised his standard at Nottingham Castle.

CHAPTER THREE

Hereford takes action

As the crisis grew nearer, there were omens and signs which to the local people had a great significance. One such occurred just north of Hereford in a meadow besides the River Lugg. Here are two large stones called the Wergins or Wirgins, one being a base on which the other stands upright. The event was described in a letter written by William Westfaling:

Sir,

My kind love and service remembred to you and your good wife, these are to let you understand of a strange thing which happened in the Wirgins upon Wednesday was sennight in the daytime about 12 of the clock, a mighty wind did drive a Stone as much as 6 Oxen could well draw six-score [yards?], and ploughed a furrow a foote and a halfe deepe all the way it went, and another Stone which 12 Oxen did draw to the Wirgins many yeares since, that stone being farre bigger than the other Stone, was carried the same time a quarter of a myle, & made no impression at all in the ground, but the Water was in the Medow a foote deepe. The bigger Stone was round and a yard and a quarter over, and about a yard deepe, the lesser Stone was a yard and a half in length, and was made fast upon the other Stone untill the wind, and I know not what did part them, there was a man of Mr. James Seabornes, which was riding to Hereford, did see one of the Stones going, and as he relates, a blacke Dog going before the Stone, the man was a great distance of and put in a greate feare, other Market people doe relate it, because I would write the truth unto you, I ridde this morning to see the Stones, and as I could guess the Stones to be carried the same distance which I have written unto you, I presume you know the Wirgins, it is the way as we ride to Sutton, and the stones were brought to the Wirgins long since, for a Marke to know the way. All your friends here are in good health, and we wish the like to you and yours. Thus praying to God to mend these miserable times, I cease.

Your loving friend,
William Westfaling

Hereford, Febr., the 23, 1641

This strange story was still well known in the early 18th century, though memory was already muddling dates. Daniel Defoe had heard about it and made enquiries when he arrived in the area. He related that 'between Sutton and Hereford, is a common meadow call'd the Wergins, where were plac'd two large stones for a water-mark; one erected upright, and the other laid a-thwart. In the late Civil Wars, about the Year 1652, they were remov'd to about twelve score paces distance, and no body knew how; which gave occasion to a common opinion, That they were carried thither by the Devil. When they were set in their places again, one of them requir'd nine yoke of oxen to draw it.'

The Wergin's stone still stands, together with its base, in a meadow alongside the road leading from Hereford towards Sutton. In a short Woolhope Club article Alfred Watkins called it a megalithic monument and dated it as being a little earlier than Stonehenge. He went on to introduce his famous Ley Line theory and suggested that the stone was on at least two leys, one going to British Camp on the Malverns, the other to Bockleton. Perhaps it was with this in mind that he chose to pour cold water on any suggestion that the stones were ever moved.

Much of the information about the build up to the Civil War comes from letters that were written at the time. One such collection was penned by Lady Brilliana Harley, the wife of Sir Robert Harley. They lived at Brampton Bryan in the extreme north-west of Herefordshire. Robert was born at Wigmore Castle in 1579 and, having gained a degree of Batchelor of Arts at Oriel College, entered the Inner Temple. He represented Radnor in Parliament during the reign of James I and continued under Charles. He was an ardent Parliamentarian and a strict Puritan, thus clashing with the majority of the gentry in Herefordshire. He was to suffer great losses during the Civil War when his house at Brampton Bryan was burnt to the

Sir Robert Harley

ground and his parks and farms plundered of all their stock. Brilliana, daughter of Sir Edward Conway of Ragley in Warwickshire, was Robert's third wife whom he married in 1623 when she was 23 and he was 44. Most of her letters, which were published for the Camden Society in 1854, are written to her son Edward who was born on 21 October, 1624. The letters are written between 1638 and 1643 when he was first at University, then in Lincoln's Inn, until, in 1642 he became captain of a troop of horse in the Parliamentarian army. The earlier letters were written to her husband who spent most of his time in London.

The earliest give some impression of the gradual build-up to the Civil War. Even in this remote part of the country, and as early as March, 1625, Brilliana wrote to her husband mentioning that 'Yesterday your company

Lady Brilliana Harley

only was at Heariford, to shewe what they had lerned, whear Sir John
Scidemore and Mr Vaughan weare judges; and so they meane to be of the
best of the companies, and they have apointed ten of your company to
learne the use of theire armes and so to teach the rest.'

By February, 1641, she was writing to her son Ned, 'in Hariford, they
have turned the tabell in the cathedrall, and taken away the cups and
bassins and all such things. I hope they begin to see that the Lord is about
to purge His church of all such invencions of men.' Such actions were
taking place throughout the country as the Puritan movement continued
to gain the support of Parliament.

A little later she referred to the rumours that were travelling the country and wrote that she much desired 'to heare how the parlament tooke the ansure of the justices of this country, that sent word they knew not by what authority the parlament did require the taking of the protestation.' This was doubtless the Protestation that was taken by the House of Commons in May, 1641, and which most members of the House signed, issuing directions that all in the country should also sign. First sheriffs and magistrates, and then, through the offices of ministers, constables, churchwardens and overseers of the poor, followed by all people 18 years of age and upwards. The Protestation referred to 'the true, reformed, Protestant religion, expressed in the Doctrine of the Church of England, against all Popery and Popish Innovations, and according to the Duty of my Allegiance to his majesty's Royal Person, Honour and Estate; as also the Power and Priviledge of Parliament, the lawful Rights and Liberties of the Subjects, and every Person that maketh this Protestation ...'

The content of the Protestation was highly offensive to most Herefordshire gentry so they arranged for an alternative to be produced specially for the county. This was known as the Herefordshire Protestation and was designed to support the king in his stance against Parliament.

To ensure that it was taken seriously it was accompanied with a rejoinder 'I doe strictly enjoyne, without exception, all commanders and souldyers, gentry, cittizens, ffree-holders and others within the county and cittye of Herefford to take this protestation, which is to be tendered unto them by the Highe Sheriffe and Comissioners of the county, assisted with such a divine as they shall make choice of to that purpose; and that a scedule of their names who shall refuse to take the same is to be delivered unto Sir William Bellendene, Comissary-Generall'.

People were being forced to declare for one side or the other.

Other petitions followed and in May, 1642, the Journal of the House of Commons noted that 'the House being informed that divers gentlemen of the County of Hereford were at the Door, who desired to present a Petition to this House: They were called in, and did present the same, and then they withdrew; and their Petition was read.' It was from 'the High Sheriffe, and divers of the Gentrey, Ministers, Freeholders, and Inhabitants of the county of Hereford' and was obviously produced at the instigation of Sir Robert Harley. The House found their petition 'full of great expressions of Duty to his Majesty, and of Love and Respects to this House and the Commonwealth (for which they give you Thanks)'. Indeed, much of it was a plea for the parliament to continue to take a strong hand on religious matters mentioning 'your Pious Care to settle a Government

THE HEREFORDSHIRE PROTESTATION

I [Name], being hereunto required doe willingly and in the presence of Almighty God solemnely vow and protest as followeth:

1. That I beleeve noe power of pope or parliament can depose the soveraigne Lo. K. Charles, or absolve mee from my naturall allegiance and obedience unto his royall person and successors.

2. That the two Howses of Parliament without the king's consent, hath noe authority to make lawes, or to bind or oblige the subject by their ordinances.

3. Wherefore I beleeve that the Earls of Essex and Manchester, Sir Tho. Fairfax, Sir Will. Waller, Col. Massie, together with all such as already have or hereafter shall take up armes by authority and commission of the members of parliament of Westminster, pretendinge to fight for Kinge and parliament, doe thereby become actuall rebells, and all such ought with their adherents and partakers to be prosecuted and brought to condigne punishment.

4. That myselfe will never beare armes in their quarrell; but if I shal be thereunto called, will assist my soveraigne and his armyes in the defence of his royall person, crowne, and dignity, against all contrary forces, unto the uttermost of my skill and power, and with the hazard of my life and fortunes.

5. That I will not discover the secretts of his Majestyes armyes to the rebells, nor hold any correspondence or intelligence with them. And all designes of theirs against our soveraignes armyes, or for surprizeinge or delivering uppe the cittyes of Worcester or Hereford, or of any other his Majestyes forts, I shall truly discover to whom it shall concern, so soon as ever it comes unto my knowledge

6. That his Majesties takeinge up of armes for the causes by himselfe so oft declared in print is just and necessary.

7. That I will endeavour all I may to hinder all popular tumults, riseings, randevous, meetings, confederancies, and associations of the people, townes, hundreds, and countyes which are not warranted to assemble by his Majesties express commission, or by power derived from him or by vertue of his commissions, and in the sense he meanes it.

8. I detest from my heart that seditious and trayterous late invented nationall covenant, and I promise never to take it.

All these particular articles I vow and promise sincerely to observe without equivocation or mentall reservation

So helpe me God.

in the Church according to the Word of God, your godly desires to prevent the Prophaning of the Lord's day, your zeal to provide Preaching Ministerie throughout the Kingdome, whereof this County stands in great neede, it now abounding with insufficient, Idle, and Scandalous Ministers, whereby the people generally are continued in Ignorance, Superstition, and Prophanenesse, and are ready to become a prey to popish seducers, which Idolatrous profession hath of late years with much boldnesse appeared in this County ...' The Petition was printed and the copy seen by Webb and quoted in his *Civil War in Herefordshire* was endorsed in Sir Robert Harley's handwriting. Although the Petition mentions the crisis in Ireland and the local problem caused by the importation of Spanish wool, the main emphasis is concerned with the strengthening of the Puritan movement and the suppression of the Laudians. The fact that it was only supported by 'Divers of the gentry' and more so the freeholders, indicates that, as a whole, the gentry were for the king, whilst the new individual holders of capital were for Parliament.

By June, 1642, Lady Brilliana was beginning to feel more than a little insecure at Brampton Bryan, surrounded as she was by Royalist gentry, and wrote to her son to say, 'Since your father thinkes Hearefordsheare as safe as any other country, I will thinke so too; but when I considered how long I had bine from him, and how this country was affected, my desire to see your father, and my care to be in a place of safety, made me earnestly desire to come up to Loundoun.' Later in the letter she wrote, 'This day Mr. Davis came from Hereford, wheare he went to preach, by the intreaty of some in the town, and this befell him: when he had ended his prayer before the sermon, which he was short in, because he was loth to tire them, two men went out of the church and cryed "Pray God bless the king; this man does not pray for the king"; upon which, before he read his text, he told them that ministers had that liberty to pray before or after the sermon for church and state. For all that, they went to the bells and rang, and a great many went into the churchyard and cryed "Roundheads", and some said "let us cast stones at him!" and he could not look out of doors, nor Mr. Lane, but they cryed "Roundhead". In the afternoon they would not let him preach, so he went to the cathedral. Those that had any goodness weare much trubled, and weepe much.'

The situation was even more serious by 17 July when she wrote, 'I sent Samuell to Heariford to obsarve their ways. He had come home last night, but that he had a fall from his hors and put out his shoulder. He tells me that they all at Heareford cried out against your father, and not one said any thinge for him, but one man, Mr. Phillips of Ledbury said, when he herd them speak so against your father, "Well" said he, "tho Sir Robert Harley be low heare, yet he is above, wheare he is." My deare Ned, I can not thinke I am safe at Brompton [Brampton Bryan], and by no meanes I would have you come downe.' She goes on to say 'I could wish that my cosen Adams were out of the howse, for I am perswaded he will give the other side what assistance he can. If you thinke good, tell your father so: your father does not know what counsells they have in Hearifordsheare, and what way they go. The captain of the voluntiers is one Barell, he was a tradesman, and once maire of Heariford.' (This presumably refers to the James Barrol who was mayor in 1639.)

It was about this time that the battle of petitions reached another climax with the publication of *The Declaration or Resolution of the County of Hereford*. Apart from listing grievances and suggesting solutions, it upheld 'the Protestant Religion, the King's just power, the Laws of the Land, and the Libertie of the Subject.' It concluded by stating 'Nor shall we ever yeeld our selves such Slaves, or so betray the liberty purchased by our Forefathers blood and bequeathed unto us, as to suffer our selves to be swayed by an Arbitary Government whatsoever, nor stand with too much contention of Spirit to cast off the Yoake of one Tyranny to endure many worse. And seeing his majestie is graciously pleased to maintaine the true Protestant Religion; His owne just Power, the Lawes of the Land, the Liberty of the Subjects, and that these waters of Reformation, having been long stirred; we want onely the favour of his Princely Majesty to let us in and heale us: So we doe reciprocally declare that we conceive our selves bound to maintaine him in all the Premisses with our Lives and Fortunes.'

It was probably circulated in June, 1642, and can be seen as a spirited reply to Sir Robert Harley's petition a month earlier. Intended as inflammatory material, it was not submitted to Parliament but instead was sold in the bookshops of the capital and by men on the streets. Copies were thus readily available and in the Commons on 8 July, 1642, Mr. Maddison said that on reading it in a stationer's shop he had observed that 'this was a foul Scandal upon the Parliament, and that the Author of it deserved to be whipt.' He was overheard by Sir William Boteler who told him that he deserved to be whipped for saying so, sentiments that were echoed by Mr. Dutton, a minister.

Mr. Dutton was called in and told by the Speaker that 'this was one of the foulest and most scanalous libels that ever was raised or published against the Parliament' and committed him to prison in the Gatehouse during the pleasure of the House. The printer and two men who were caught selling the paper were committed to Newgate.

One of the most interesting of the local commentaries concerning this period is in the account book of Joyce Jefferies who was resident in Herefordshire throughout the Civil War. Joyce Jefferies was the daughter of Henry Jefferies of Homme-castle in the parish of Clifton-on-Teme, and Anne, widow of James Coningsby. Following her father's death, she lived with her mother at Cotheridge, some 4 miles west of Worcester. When her mother died she was invited to move to Hampton Court in north Herefordshire, the home of Sir Thomas Coningsby, where she became companion to Philippa, Sir Thomas's wife. She had recieved 200 marks on her father's death and with this and by various other benefactions and gratuities, her income eventually reached a peak of some £900 per annum. This was sufficient to make her totally independent and she eventually describes herself as a resident of Hereford.

The account book covers a nine year period beginning in 1638. She lived in the city until 1642 when she sought refuge with friends in the countryside. She finally gave up keeping her own house in 1644 when she moved in with relatives. The book is inscribed:

A New Booke of Receights of Rents, Anuities,
and Interest Moneys begininge at St. Mary Day, 1638:
written at Heryford at John Fletcher's howse.

An entry in the book establishes that John Fletcher's house was in the part of Widemarsh Street that was outside the gate. According to her great-nephew, Henry Jefferies, she built 'a house in Wigmarsh Street in the suburbs of Hereford', costing over £500. It has since been established that her new house was on the western side of Widemarsh Street, where the multi-storey car park now stands. Joyce Jefferies had other properties in Widemarsh Street, all apparently outside the gate, and all let to tenants.

The entries in her diary give a vivid impression of the gradual build-up of tension at the beginning of the Civil War:

1638: May 1	Paid Mr. Mailard, mercer, and John Trahern, shoe-maker, for the shipping money for this year	£3
	Paid ship-money for 15 acres of grainge land by Leominster	2s. 6d.
1638: Nov. 26	Paid towards the king's povysion for the same land	2d.

James Wathen's sketch of the outside of Widemarsh Gate in 1790

1639: March 26 Paid John Trahern, my sowldier, 3 days'
               training   5s.
Midsummer   For watching one night at Widemarsh Gate 2s.

By this time trained bands were being called out and exercised, the costs being borne by the local landowners. Precautions were also being taken to prevent mischief by having regular guards, but this did not stop soldiers, or those pretending to be soldiers, from wandering in the streets, begging or obtaining money by threats or through fear:

1639: Sept. 5 Gave a strainge sowldier, with a blue feather in
               his hat, that said he came from barrick   2s.
Oct. 24 Gave a counterfett sowldier or a theef rather
                                                            4d.

When the king raised his army of some 20,000 men to quell the Scots, some of Mrs Jefferies' relatives and friends must have agreed to go. They needed funds and provisions and came to her for help.

> 1640 April 2 Gave Mr Miles Hackluit when he went to the
> warres against Scottland   2s. 6d.
> Gave my cosin Will Coningsby when he went to
> Scottland to the warres   1s.
> July 10 This day the trained sowldiers went towards
> Scottland. Gave John Lincoln that went with
> Captain Button   6d.
> Gave 3 sowldiers of ye same company to drink 4d.

She had similar commitments throughout 1640, paying £3 to 'James Barrell', the mayor, for Ship Money, having her soldier trained, and helping to pay for the watch at Widemarsh Gate. Generally things were quiet in Hereford in 1641, but the situation in the country as a whole was of considerable concern and Mrs. Jefferies took an interest, sending for various pamphlets and booklets:

> 1641: Oct 29 Paid for a booke of ye Earle of Straford's arrain-
> ment and his pickture, & ye Arch Bishop Laud's
> and som other picktures   4s. 1d.

By early the following year there were sporadic acts of violence and some damage to property. Apparently on Ascension Day, soldiers were discharging their muskets in the streets. This was also the day that Richard Weaver, of Above Eign, one of the two Members of Parliament for Hereford, was buried in Hereford Cathedral. Mrs. Jefferies apparently played for safety, but must have suffered some concern:

> 1642: May 18 Gave the sowldiers that shott off at my
> window   1s. and beer.

The Civil War officially started on 22 August, 1642, and by 9 September, the Earl of Essex, commanding some 15,000 men for Parliament, had left London bound for Northampton and the west of England. The city had to look towards its own defence:

> 1642: Sept 4 Paid to Mr Mailard, mercer in heriford, by a
> lewne [assessment] laid upon ye Citty of hery-
> ford, towards ye biinge of Armor & weapons &
> artilery to streinthen the citty against the
> parliament   20s.

> Sept 20   I paid John Trahern my sowldier for ye Citty of
> heriford, 7 daies training with his captain, Mr.
> Rich. Wigmore   10s.

When Mrs. Jefferies heard that Essex was approaching Worcester, she decided it was time to leave Hereford. In great haste she moved, first to her cousin Penreece's house at Kilkington, some ten miles west of Hereford, and then, some four days later, to Garnons, the home of her friend Francis Geers:

> 1642: Sept 23   I cam to kilkinton to my cosin penreeses howse
> from heriford for feare of ye parliaments army,
> Septem. 23, 1642.
> The 27   I came from thence to Mr Geers at Garnons.
> Paid Edward Parsons of heryford for helpping to
> carry my goods out of my howse in heriford to
> the cart that brought hit to Kilkinton, for feare
> of ye coming of ye parliaments army from
> Worcester to heriford   1s.
> Gave an other man for helpping in the same
> work   3d.
> Paid Edward Stefens, Carier, for cariing a way
> my trunks & boxes and bedding from heriford
> to kilkinton   25s.

Her help with the defences of Hereford was obviously limited to cash payments. Her personal property was her own problem and she had to pay out some money to save her belongings:

> Gave a carpinder to pass over my standard
> powles in ye cole howse, when the souldiers
> would had them to barricade Widmarsh gate 4d.

This entry probably referred to an event just before her flight from Hereford. Not surprisingly, the account book contains somewhat confused entries around this date. Joyce Jefferies continued to enter up her account book throughout the Civil War, returning to Hereford from time to time.

CHAPTER FOUR

The attack by the Earl of Stamford

There had been relatively little change in Hereford as a whole in the hundred years since John Leland's visit. Lord Clarendon, who visited the city a few years before hostilities commenced, described it as being 'a town very well affected, and reasonably well fortified, having a strong stone wall about it, and some cannon, and there being in it soldiers of good reputation, many gentlemen of honour and quality, and three or four hundred soldiers, besides the inhabitants well armed.'

During the course of the Civil War, Sir Henry Slingsby also visited Hereford and entered the following description in his diary: 'This City of Hereford is cituated not much unlike to Yorke, & in some parts resembles it very much; for it hath a round tower mount'd upon a Hill, like to Clifford's tower, & ye mills near it, with some little works about, having ye river Wye running close by; but ye walls tho' they be high yet are not mounted upon a Rampier as York walls are.'

Despite its high walls, all was not as well as the city's defenders may have wished, as is apparent from a footnote in Webb's *Civil War in Herefordshire*. He noted that 'It appears from the Corporation and other records that the gates of the city had been suffered to go to decay in the reign of King James. In the autumn of 1614 the south-west corner of Eign gate and the cracks and crevices of it were repaired by an assessment; and in 1619 St. Owen's gate was restored by the city for the purpose of containing the magazine.'

In the early 1600's, each county had a militia or trained band of foot soldiers, argument over the control of which being one of the matches which sparked the Civil War—in Royalist Herefordshire it was effectively under the command of a royal Commission of Array. The militia needed armaments and each county had a magazine containing military stores and equipment and sometimes the officers' armour. The Herefordshire magazine was held in St. Owen's Gate and an inventory taken in 1626, at the beginning of Charles's reign, gives an indication of the value of such a store to any army. According to the armourer, it contained 1,206 pounds of powder, 926 of match, and 3,928 of lead—apparently a normal amount for that magazine.

Whilst the magazine building may have been repaired, the castle was a totally different problem. To help raise money the king had sold the castle, complete with its keep on its artificial mound, and it was in the hands of an individual by the name of Page. It was apparent that it could not be used for any form of defence unless and until some considerable works of restoration had been organised and carried out. Fears for the city's defence grew as news of Essex's westward advance travelled before him.

Essex had rapidly taken Northampton then, appreciating that the king had moved from Nottingham towards Shrewsbury, countered by moving across Warwickshire into Worcestershire. Essex took Worcester and shortly afterwards his troops were involved in a sudden skirmish at Powick Bridge, just outside the city, with a Royalist detachment under the control of Prince Rupert. The parliamentarian troops were defeated, in what was the first real contact between the two warring sides, and had to retreat to Worcester.

In Worcester, Essex heard that Hereford had neither governor nor garrison and sent Henry, Earl of Stamford, to take the city. Thus, on 30 September, within six weeks of the king raising his standard at Nottingham, the city of Hereford was attacked. The official parliamentary record reads: 'Information was given to the House by letters, that 340 soldiers were come out of Herefordshire to his Excellency the Earl of Essex to serve the King and Parliament; and that the City of Hereford had sent to his Excellency stating their good affections to the Parliament, and their desire to be secured against the Cavaliers, whom they much feared would come thither, and there being a malignant party in the City, those that were well affected durst not shew their kindness as much as they would. Whereupon his Excellency sent 1,000 foot and four troops of horse to disarm the malignants, and to settle that City in a good posture of defence, and likewise ordered that a garrison should be left there for the peace and safety of their party.'

When this army arrived in Hereford it had a mixed reception as can be seen from the following letter which was the last of a series written by

Hereford Castle, as it may then have appeared, from the top of St. Owen's Gate

Nehemiah Wharton, a subaltern officer of the Earl of Essex's army. He had started his working life as an apprentice in London and had been sent by his 'master and honoured friend', as were hundreds of others, with a pocketful of money and a scriptural blessing, 'to live and die with the Earl of Essex.' There is no record of Wharton's actions after this letter, which was written to his old master in London. It was sent from Worcester and is dated 7 October, 1642.

MOST WORTHY SIR,

Fryday, Sept. 30th, was my last unto you. This day a company of knights, gentlemen, and yeomen of the county of Hereford, came to his Excelency, petitioners for strength to be sent spedily to Hereford, and forthwith we were commanded to draw out fifteen out of every company in our regiments, in all about nine hundred, with three troopes of horse and two peeces of ordinance, with which we marched (a forlorne hope) [storming party] towards Hereford: our leaders were the Earle of Stamforde, Sargeant-Major Barrif, and Captaine Inglesby, of Colonell Hampden's Re(giment), Captaine Jones of Cholmley's Re. Captaine Ward of Stamforde, Captaine Pony of Hollis his regiment, besides leiftenants and serjeants, our ministers, Mr. John Sedgwick and Mr. Kemme. After we had marched ten miles we came to Bromyard, the wether wet, and the way very fowle: here we got a little refreshment, and from hence marched ten miles further to Hereford, but very late before we got thither, and by reason of the raine and snow, and extremity of cold, one of our soildiers died by the way; and it is wonderfull wee did not all perish, for the cowardly Cavalleers were within few miles of us.

In this poore condition comminge to Hereford, the gates were shut against us, and for two houres we stood in dirt and water up to the middle legge, for the city were all malignants, save three, which were Roundheads, and the Marquesse of Harford had sent them word the day before that they should in no wise let us in, or if they did we would plunder their houses, murder their children, burne their Bibles, and utterly ruinate all, and promised he would relieve them himself with all speede; for which cause the citizens were resolved to oppose us unto the death, and having in the city three peeces of ordinance, charged them with neyles, stones &c., and placed them against us, and wee against them, resolvinge either to enter the city or dye before it.

But the Roundheads in the city, one of them an alderman, surnamed Lane, persuaded the silly mayor (for so hee is indeed) that his Excellency and all his forces weere at hand, wherupon he opened unto us, and we entered the city at Bysters Gate, but found the dores shut, many of the people with their children fled, and had enuffe to do to get a little quarter. But the poor mayor (seeinge he was so handsomely cozened) was not a little angry, for Harford, with his forces which fled from Sherborn, promised to visit them the day followinge. This night, though weet and weary, wee were faine to guard the city ...

Saturday our squadron watched at St. Owen's Gate, which day I tooke an opportunity to view the city, which is well scituate, and seated upon the river Y, environed with a strong wall, better than any I have seene before; with five gates, and a stronge stone bridge of sixe arches over the river, surpassing Worcester. In the city there is the statelyest market place in the kingdome, built with cullumnes, after the manner of the Exchange. The Minster every way exceeded that of Worcester, but the city in circuit not so large. The inhabitants are totally ignorant in the waies of God, and much addicted to drunkkenness and other vices, but principally unto swearinge, so that the children that have scarce learned to speake doe universally sweare stoutlye. Many here speake Welsh.

Sabbath day, about the time of morninge prayer, we went to the Minster, when the pipes played and the puppets sange so sweetely, that some of our soildiers could not forbeare dauncinge in the holie quire; whereat the Baalists[1] were sore displeased. The anthem ended, they fell to prayer, and prayed devoutly for the Kinge, the bissops, &c.; and one of our soildiers, with a loud voice, saide, "What! neiver a bit for the Parliament?" which offended them much more. Not satisfied with this humane service, we went to devine; and, passing by, found shops open, and men at wirke, to whom we gave some plaine exhortations; and went to heare Mr. Sedgwick, who gave us two famous sermons[2], which much affected the poore inhabi-

---

1 Those who believe in a false god—presumably the soldiers saw much evidence of popery in the cathedral
2 Quoted in Webb, Vol. 1, p.181-85

tants, who, wonderinge, said they neiver heard the like before; and I beleeve them. The Lord moove your harts to commiserate the distressers, and to send them some faithfull and painfull ministers; for the revenewe of the Collidge will maintaine many of them. This even, the Earle of Stamford (who is made governor of Hereford) entred the city with a regiment of foote and some troopes of horse, and tooke up the bishop's pallace for his quarter, and is resolved there to abide; whereupon, on Munday morning, we marched towards Worcester, and, at the end of ten miles, came to Bromyard, where we quartered the night. This day his Excelency proclaimed that all soildiers that would set to diginge should have twelve pence the day, and enter into pay presently. Tuesday we marched to Worcester, and were received with much joy, for the deseigne was so desperate that our juditious frends neiver looked to see us againe ...

Your antient, humble, and affectionate servant,
NEHEMIAH WHARTON

Included in Stamford's army were Lieut-Col Edward Massey, who was a veteran from the continent and the armies of Holland; Sergeant Major Constance Ferrer, who had once held a Captain's commission under the king, and Captain Hammond (who was to become governor of Carisbrook Castle at the time when the king was imprisoned there). Also present were Sir Robert Harley of Brampton Bryan and his eldest son, Edward; Sir Richard Hopton of Canon Frome, a magistrate; and Sergeant-Major Kirle of Ross.

Nehemiah Wharton's rather dismissive description of the mayor as 'silly' was probably an appropriate explanantion to give to the troops, but it may have been far from the truth. Other people evidently thought that there was some treachery on the part of the mayor as is shown by the following extract: 'Hereford was sold by that perfidious mayor, Price, who was Mayor of this City when the Earl of Stamford was there, a Godfather (if he did not take the name in vain) to his child then newly born, who desired his Lordship to name the baby "Parliament", but consulting with the mother, it was declined because it had not then been resolved upon the question, whether "Parliament" were a christian name.'

Soon, rumours of a counter-attack began to spread. One pamphlet stated that Charles was outside the walls of Hereford on Saturday 7 October with 2,000 men and was refused admission. This was totally spurious for all the evidence indicates that the king was in Shrewsbury at that date.

However, by November the Royalists were attempting by all means possible to threaten Stamford in Hereford and had occupied what was described as a 'fort' some 7 or 8 miles from the city. This was possibly at the Mynd, the home of Sir Walter Pye, a noted Royalist, in the parish of Much Dewchurch. From there, at the end of November, a small boy arrived at Hereford with a note for Sergeant-Major Ferrar. It read:

> Sir,
> My good Opinion of you makes me believe that your Necessity, rather than your Will, hath made you One in this Rebellion. My Affection to you finds a Way to bring you out of both; which may thus be done: We shall suddenly approach to Hereford with such Forces as will (God willing) soon reduce the Rebels in it to the King's Mercy. If you, in that mean Time, will contrive now to advantage us in this Design, his Excellency hath commanded me to offer you Five Hundred Pounds in Money, and to assure both yourself and your Assistants not only of your Pardons, but that you shall be preferred to better Charges in his Majesty's Army than you have. Sir, bethink yourself betimes, and return your Answer by the Bearer, that I may confidently stile myself, Sir,
> Your most hearty Friend to serve you,
> R. LAWDEY

The writer was Sir Richard Lawdey of Exeter, who had been created a baronet a fortnight before and held the rank of Colonel (later Major-general) in Lord Herbert's army. Previously he had served with Ferrar in the king's army to Scotland and must have considered the attempt at subversion worthwhile. Bribes were not uncommon at that time and were sometimes successful, though apparently not in this case, for Constance Ferrar replied:

> Sir,
> I received a Letter that bears your Name, inviting me to such an Act of Baseness as (these must tell you) I hold in highest Disdain; for never yet did my Necessity (or ever shall) put me one Tittle off my Fidelity, or inforce me to violate my Honour, which, not withstanding the large Offer you make from his Excellency, I shall still endeavour (as hitherto I have done) entirely to preserve. As for his Majesty's Pardon, I conceive not

myself to stand in Need of it, my Service and Employment being only for the Preservation of the true Protestant Religion, the Safety of his Majesty's Person, the Defence of the Laws of the Land, the Liberty of the Subject, and Privilege of Parliament; whereunto, I am persuaded, all true-hearted Englishmen are conscientiously obliged. For your undoubted Power to reduce the Rebels in Hereford (as you term them), doubt not, Sir, when you come, you shall receive the entertainment of a Soldier.
CONSTANCE FERRAR
Hereford, Dec. the 1st. 1642

Bearing in mind that regular pay for the army was far from guaranteed and that food was scarce, the temptation to accept a substantial bribe such as the one offered must have been considerable. Indeed, the character of Ferrar was not above suspicion. According to one of his enemies, when Ferrar was in Gloucester, where he was Town-Major, a few days before the city's investment, he was spoken of as open to a similar temptation 'soe hee may save what hee hath gotten.' At a later date he was suspected by Parliament and his honesty was questioned by Massey. He was sent to London and detained in custody from 17 May to 21 Aug, 1644, and only released to be discharged from his employment at Gloucester. Even after this rejection, he returned to the army and was ultimately killed in the service of Parliament at Banbury.

Joyce Jefferies continued to compile her account book and, although she had moved out of the city, was sufficiently close to be aware of events. The army under Stamford's control had officers who were fresh from the German wars and experienced in pilfering, or plundering as it became known. It was said that they pillaged 'all that kep faith and allegeance with the King' and promised to keep them so short of food that they would 'eate the very flesh from their arms.'

Mrs. Jefferies made a bad choice in staying at Garnons, for Mr. Geers's house was one of those singled out by the parliamentarian troops. She wrote:

1642: 30 Sept.   The parliaments army cam to heriford from Worster, Henry Gray, Earle of Stamford, ye Generall. On Tewsday morning, October 4, captain Hamon [Hammond] and his barbarous company plundered Mr. Geereses howse at Garnons, both them and me of much Goods, toke a way my 2 bay coache mares and som

> money, and much Linen: and Elyza Acton's
> clothes. I cam from Garnons ye same Tuesday
> to Mr. John Garbinder's to Hinton [in Norton
> Canon], a mile off, and staied there till the 14
> of December following. I lent Mr. Francis Geers
> ye younger to goe in to Wales, after his fathers
> house was plundered and a man kild   40s.

She seems to have been safe at Hinton, but moved back to Garnons on 14 December, the day that Stamford marched out of Hereford and the Royalists took possession again. She then managed to retrieve some of the belongings she had lost:

> 1643: Jan 7   Gave goody Lawrence for keeping clothes of
>   myne and Eliza Actons in ye hill for feare of ye
>   plunders   1s.
>   Paid Mathias Rufford [her steward], which he
>   laaied out to redeeme my 2 black bever Hatts,
>   and 2 gould bands out of ye theeffes, or plun-
>   derers hand, they took at Garnons   21s. 6d.

She had to resolve several problems in Hereford for soldiers had been quartered in her house. Apparently she had left some maid-servants there with Eliza Acton in charge. Messages must have been sent to her from Hereford for:

> 1642 Nov 30   I sent Bess Newton by Thos. Harris to bye
>   pvision for 4 souldiers that dietted at my howse
>   10s.

A few days earlier she had been successful in selling some 'barley mault' to 'Mrs Jane Higgings of Heriford, widdow and bruer'. She sold it 'for feare of the earle of Stanford's plundering of my howses in heriford, which hee did most in humanely'. There must have been a considerable amount of malt for she received £14 3s. 4d. for it. She even managed to get some of her belongings back:

> 1642   Paid ye man of ye fethers for 4 cariges of my
>   boords from the Lord Stanford's lodging at Mrs.
>   Wardins howse in Heriford   2s.

Throughout the whole period that he was in control in Hereford the Earl of Stamford had problems in paying and feeding his large army. Throughout the city, food was in short supply and very costly. Stamford had borrowed to the hilt and, although he had had help from Sir Robert Harley, he had to attempt to raise a loan in the city. William Price, the mayor, subscribed £40 and persuaded some others to follow. However, the response was very poor, for the majority of the citizens were opposed to the garrison and were not prepared to help. Price was a mercer of some respectability and influence among the townsmen; he was described as being of great integrity and with London connections. It was perhaps by virtue of his office, but more likely from a secret leaning towards their cause, that he was one of the few who exerted himself to accommodate the troops in Hereford. He was eventually to suffer for his beliefs.

The problems were highlighted in a dispatch from Stamford in which he said: 'I am confident the Parliament hath so well accepted of my poor Endeavours, since it hath pleased God to prosper me in all my Proceedings hitherto to be such a Gall and Impediment to their Design; for I am confident, had I not kept this unworthy City, a Torrent of Papists and Malignants had fallen down, which might have augmented the Adversaries to an infinite number. Now, my Lord, we have as much Heart and Courage left us as ever we had; but we have neither Monies nor Credit for Bread, our Hay and Provender being very scant; yet, so long as I can find any Means of Subsistence, I shall remain here. The county, as well as this vile city, are so base and malignant, that, although the roguish Army of the Welch Papists, and other Vagabonds, that were beaten in the First Battle in Warwickshire, do plunder, kill, murder, and destroy Men and Women, take away all their Goods and Cattle; yet, such is their Hatred to our Condition, that they had rather be so used and illtreated, than to be rescued or relieved by us.'

The situation gradually deteriorated, especially when the royal forces occupied Worcester, and Stamford must have felt himself all but surrounded by his enemy. The only route left open to him was south-eastwards to Gloucester and on 14 December[3], 1642, having held Hereford for some ten weeks, Stamford decided that he had no choice but to abandon the city. In this he had to act on his own responsibility for communications were, to say the least, difficult and slow. Although he was in receipt of a commission by which, in the absence of the Earl of Essex, he was commander in chief of all the forces raised in the counties of

---

3 Some authorities say that the troops were withdrawn on 3 December

Hereford, Gloucester, Worcester and Shropshire, this meant little, for there was little possibility of raising an army in these remote and largely Royalist areas without any useful contacts. For a short while the counties of Worcester and Hereford were both in Royalist hands.

Shortly after the parliamentarian troops left the city, Sir Richard Lawdey and his detachment moved in. The occupation had demonstrated that there were people in Hereford prepared to aid and abet the parliamentarian cause and, once Stamford had left, these people could be publically proclaimed traitors and suitably penalised. Troops were sent into the country areas around the city seeking retaliation against all who had supported the recent occupying army. Several people were brought back to Hereford to be incarcerated in the bishop's prison, others suffered considerable loss of possessions and damage to property.

Colonel Fitz-William Coningsby of Hampton Court had been appointed by the king as Sheriff of the County and later as one of the Commissioners of Array. On 20 December he recieved an official appointment by commission from the Marquess of Hertford and became 'Gouvernor of the Cittee and Garrison of Hereford as touchinge the Militia'. This commanded all officers and soldiers of that garrison, and 'all other person and persons whatsoever whom it may concern', to obey him in that capacity. Fitz-William Coningsby was the son of Sir Thomas Coningsby who, in 1613, had founded the Coningsby Hospital in Widemarsh Street, Hereford, for aged soldiers, mariners and serving-men. At the rear, he had converted part of the old Blackfriars monastery as his town house and this would doubtless have been used by his son. He would thus have been a near neighbour as well as cousin of Joyce Jefferies.

Coningsby was given the problem of raising sufficient money to pay for the new garrison, for there were no funds available. He achieved this by a regular assessment and Mrs. Jefferies helped both with the quota and with voluntary contributions. She was ill in December and spent the whole of the winter at Garnons:

> 1642 Dec 27   I sent my good friend Mr ffrancis Geeres ye
> younger to Mr. Coningesby to pay souldiers at
> heriford as a present   £50
> and a fatt bullock worth £6 also of a present

By Christmas, Mr. Coningsby had also sent a letter to Brilliana Harley via Mr. Wigmore of Lucton. On the same day she wrote to her son, who was then in London with his father, 'I did not let him come into my howse, but

I went into the garden to him. Your father will sheawe you the letter; they are in a mighty violence against me; they reveng all that was doune upon me, so that I shall fear any more parlament forsess comeing into this cuntry.' She goes on to ask him to discuss with his father 'wheather he thinkes it best that I should put away most of the men that are in my howses, and wheather it be best for me to go from Brampton, or by God's healp to stand it out?'

The outside of Eign Gate in 1784

CHAPTER FIVE

The assault by William Waller

When the parliamentarian troops left Hereford in December 1642, the city entered into a short period of peace—a period in which the citizens should have taken the opportunity offered to repair the defences of the city and restore the castle to the strong point it had once been. The city ditch needed cleaning out to ensure that it held a good depth of water; the city gates needed repair to withstand the cannons of any attacker and draw-bridges were needed to prevent a direct attack on the gates. The river frontage was open to approach by boat and needed additional defensive works, particularly along the edge of the castle. But the most important requirement was one which could not be taken easily—the demolition of all buildings outside the gates which could conceal anyone attacking the city.

But nothing was done to improve the defensive capability of the city—the Militia may have been well trained, but Hereford was just as undefensible when William Waller arrived outside the gate in April, 1643, as it had been when the Earl of Stamford left in the previous December.

Whilst Stamford was still at Hereford, Charles had made an attempt to move towards London. Because of this, Essex had to move his main army from Worcester to stay between the king and the capital and, as both armies manoeuvred, each some 15,000 strong, they drew closer together. They eventually met at the Battle of Edgehill on 23 October, 1642. Although the result was indecisive, the Royalists failed in their attempt to reach London and had to be satisfied with taking Banbury, before retreating to Oxford for the winter.

In the midlands, the king held sway through Oxfordshire into Staffordshire and along the Welsh border, whilst the Roundheads were supreme in Derbyshire, Northamptonshire, Warwickshire and Gloucester-shire. Leicestershire and Nottinghamshire were split; in the latter Newark was Royalist whilst Nottingham, where Charles had originally raised his standard, was now held by Parliament.

The winter was a quiet period throughout much of the country, but some attempts were made to consolidate positions and stake claims to adjoining areas. One of the main efforts was in the south of the region where Sir William Waller had a resounding success at the Battle of Highnam, not far from Gloucester. Waller's string of successes continued and, in the early spring of 1643 he left Gloucester on his way towards Hereford. He had apparently had some secret information to the effect that the defences of Hereford were still as weak as they had been when Stamford captured the city. Indeed, one of Waller's staff officers, Lieutenant-Colonel Massey, had served under Stamford and knew Hereford reasonably well. He supplied Waller with information about the state of the defences of the city and considered that the Welsh levies, which formed part of the garrison, were not very reliable and that the officers were of poor quality. The information was sufficient to convince Waller that an attack was practicable. He came with some 2,500 men from Ross through Fownhope and arrived at dawn on 25 April. His information and advice had been correct, and after a minor bombardment and a few sallies, the authorities agreed to parley and eventually surrendered. Waller had succeeded in taking the city 'with the loss of one man and the hurt of three or four soldiers.'

The date is well verified by an entry in the Baptism Register at St. Peter's church: 'Edward Jones, ye sonne of Edward Jones and Elizabeth, his wife, was born ye 23rd April 1643 and was baptized ye 25th of April 1643, ye same month which day come to ye city of Hereford Sir William Waller.'

There is a short description of the action by Mr. Corbett, a minister from Gloucester, who was with Sir William Waller's army. He wrote:

> The main body of the horse and foot were drawn up before Bister's gate on the North side of the Town, and stood aloof and shot at random, till Waller commanded Captain Grey with a party of musqueteers over the river towards the Wye bridge, whose march was secured by a rising bank under the walls. These were ordered to make a show of an assault, and if need were, to fall back into the water side, where seconds were placed for their relief—The enemies horse sallied out upon them, whom that party having gallantly kept off, and forced back into the City

withdrew thence and gained a church within pistol shot of St. Owen's gate, whence our musqueteers played on the walls. [This would have been St. Owen's Church.] To help forward the capture of the City, Massie drew up two sakers[1] in a straight line against Wide Marsh gate, not without extreme hazard of being shot from the walls, and himself gave fire, and the first cannon-shot entered the gate and took an officer's head from his shoulders and slew some besides. More shots were made, each of which scoured the street and so alarmed the enemy that they presently sounded a parley which was entertained by Sir W. Waller.'

All this had taken place between dawn on the 25th and three o'clock in the afternoon. Had there been a spark of resistance from the defenders, Waller would have had to retreat, for he was at that very moment under orders to join the Earl of Essex and to assist in the siege of Reading.

Lord Clarendon also provided a short description of the city and clearly shows his surprise that it had been taken so easily. Of Waller he wrote 'He came before Hereford, a town very well affected, and reasonably well fortified, having a strong stone wall about it and some cannon, there being in it some soldiers of good reputation, and many gentlemen of honour and quality, with three or four hundred soldiers, besides the inhabitants well armed; yet without the loss of one man on either side, to the admiration of all who then heard it, or ever since heard of it, he perswaded them fairly to give up the town, and yield themselves prisoners upon quarter, which they did, and were presently sent by him for their better security to Bristol.'

The surprise was even greater in other parts of the country. The *Court Mercury* recorded:

Munday May 1—This day the newes that Sir William Waller had taken Hereford, was confirmed for certaine. It had been certified before on Friday last, and the same day crossed; reported doubtfully on Saturday, according as men stood affected to the parties, who were suspected not to have done their best endeavours in it; and not affirmed with any confidence on Sunday. The reasons why it was surrendered, and the condition that the Towne was in when it was given up, being yet in question, may be imparted at another time when the case is clearer; and that it be discovered evidently where the fault did lie.

---

1 A saker was a cannon, 3.5 inches in diameter and 9 feet long. The shot weighed 6lbs. and required 4lbs. of powder

Sir William Waller, by an unknown artist

The first glimmerings of suspicion were being raised—had someone betrayed the city and if so who? Could they be suitably punished? The suspicion grew and Secretary Nicholls wrote to the Marquess of Ormond from Oxford, where the Royalists were based, to say: 'There hath been lately two very considerable towns, [Reading and Hereford] rendered to the rebels here, as is strongly suspected, by trechery; for we heare that since they cannot prevayle against his Majestie's forces, they say they will make tryall what they can doe by corrupting some of our commanders ... '

The story rapidly grew more complex and, according to *Speciall Passages* for May 3, a bribe of £3,000 was paid to someone. However, in the *Perfect Diurnall* for May 4 this was explained as: 'The Citizens have compounded with Sir Willm. Waller for £3000, to be exempted from plundering.'

William Price, perhaps surprisingly, had not yet been replaced as mayor of the city and was again of help to the parliamentarian forces, this time in the collection of the ransom. A note signed by Waller records that: 'I do hearby certifie on the behalfe of William Price of Hereford, that when I was there in the yeare 1643 he beeinge Major did in his place use mee respectively, and whatt fine was then laid upon the City, he willingly afforded his best endeavours for ceaseinge [assessing] & collectinge the same: and to my best remembrance ther was Twenty pounds paid by him towards this said fine.'

This was not the only attempt at ransom, for one of Waller's officers, a Colonel Cary, was paid the not inconsiderable sum of £6 3s. 4d. by the parish of All Saints to redeem the bells, which were evidently considered forfeit. This must have been in late April, 1643. Although more common in Germany, it was unusual, if not unique, for a ransom to be demanded for bells. There is no mention of a similar ransom in the accounts for St. Nicholas Church despite those bells being rung for Royalist victories as often as those of All Saints. Was All Saints a special case? The near loss of the bells did not stop the churchwardens from carrying out their duty to keep them in good condition and later in 1643 John Finch, the Hereford bell-founder, repaired four of the wheels and provided one new one. The bells were rung as usual on 5 November that year.

Joyce Jefferies continued to record her various payments and the events in Hereford in her account book. Her cousin, Fitz-William Coningsby, who had been appointed governor of Hereford in December, 1642, was captured by Sir William Waller at the end of March, 1643, when he was part of the army raised by Lord Herbert of Raglan in an attempt to retake Gloucester. Following this Colonel Herbert Price was appointed to succeed Coningsby as governor. Early in April, Joyce Jefferies returned to Hereford to visit her 'new house', but Waller's impending approach drove her away again and she returned to her friends in the Garnons area on 20 April. She moved some of her belongings:

1643 April 20   Paid the man of the fethers in Heriford for
                 bringing ... trunks and ... cheste from Heriford
                 to George Edwards howse in Little Mansell to
                 keepe   6s.

When Waller came to Hereford on 25 April 1643, the main focus of his attack was on Widemarsh Gate, close to where Joyce Jefferies had her various houses. The attack there was little more than a scuffle and caused little damage to the buildings. Mrs. Jefferies noted the event:

> 1643 April 24 he cam, and 25 Wensday, &c. he entered ye
> citty. Paid John Baddam for mending ye tile
> over my new closett, which Sir Willm. Waller's
> sowldiers brake downe to shote at Widemarsh
> gate when he besieged ye citty of heriford 4d.

The contributions that Sir William Waller insisted on having from the citizens to prevent their houses being plundered varied according to their means. Mrs. Jefferies had to pay £40; only three other householders in the whole city were assessed as high. Even so, some plundering took place and Mrs. Jefferies was one of those to suffer:

> 1643 Paid Richard Winnye, smith, for mending lokes
> and kayes at heriford which the plunderrs
> broke   16d.
> Paid Maud Pritchet for a cheese when Sir
> Willm Waller was in Heriford for his sowldiers
> that I kept   18d.

She must have felt much safer staying with her relatives at Garnons rather than in her house in Hereford, for she did not come back even when Waller had left. It was not until April, 1644, that she returned to her new house, and even then she only stayed for a couple of days.

The loss of Hereford without any real effort to defend the city was a great blow to the Royalist cause. It is quite probable that this hasty surrender was in part due to the consternation that prevailed as a result of Waller's defeat of Herbert near Gloucester, but a scapegoat had to be found. Sir Richard Cave, who held a commission in the king's cavalry, was involved with the defence of Hereford just before and during the attack on the city. He also managed to escape when many 'men of note, quality, and good estate', who were in Hereford at the time, were captured. As a result, when he arrived in Oxford, he was immediately put under arrest and charged with dishonourably giving up the city.

Cave had to produce a written defence and fortunately this has survived. It gives an excellent picture of his experiences. The first section describes the events that led up to his arrival in Hereford. He explained that, at the king's command, he had waited on Prince Maurice at Tewkesbury. On 9 April he was dispatched to South Wales to encourage resistance there and help encircle Waller at Gloucester. He was provided with 'about eighty horse and about one hundred dragoones, to which I was to joine (as occasion served), three companies of Colonel Herbert Price's regiment (whereof two laid at Abergavenny and ye third at Hereford), and about an hundred of Colonel Coningsby's regiment.'

He was obviously successful for by 11 April he had possessed himself of Monmouth 'and was ready from thence to have fallen upon Sir William Waller as his Highness' marches and further commands should have given occasion.' By this time Waller was nearly surrounded, but he managed to cut his way free without coming across Sir Richard Cave. With no-one to attack, Cave expected to return, but Prince Maurice had other ideas and commanded him 'to unite ye forces of Hereford, Monmouth, and South Wales' in an effort to gain a sufficient force to take Gloucester.

He was again successful and set up a meeting at Abergavenny where the commissioners from the chosen counties met with Lord Herbert who was in charge of the whole area. It was apparent that Herbert had some doubts about the reliability of his new allies, but it was agreed that the various forces should rendezvous at Hereford. After some persuasion by Cave, Lord Herbert agreed to attend and 'on Tuesday ye 18th April, came to Hereford, within three miles of which towne Lieutenant-Colonel Howell Gwin quartered with about 140 or 150 of my Lord Herbert's men, who did, according to my Lord's fformer doubt, disband ye next morning, leaving theire armes behind them, which ye Lieutenant-Colonel loaded into cartes and carrid away.'

On 22 April, at about ten o'clock at night, Cave received the long-awaited command from Prince Maurice for his instant return. This was the day that 'Sir William Waller moved towards Rosse, and wee were advertized as much; and ye same evening my Lord Herbert went from Hereford to Mr. More's house[2], 4 miles from ye towne, whither I sent immediately a letter directed unto him from ye Prince, and the copy of his Highness' letter to me.'

Although it was apparent that Waller was likely to move from Ross towards Hereford, Lord Herbert refused all requests to stay and command the forces defending the city. Cave said that Herbert was 'seeming to require me (which he had no power to doe, especially being recalled) to take that charge.' This left Cave in a quandary. Should he abandon

---

2 Presumably William More of Burghope, Wellington, who died in 1657.

Hereford and return to the prince or should he stay with his small force and help with the defence. His final decision, made 'upon the extraordinary importunity of my Lord Scudamore, Sir William Croft, Sir Walter Pye, Colonel Herbert Price, and others,' was 'to stay there as an assistant, to contribute ye best of my service to ye maine end for which his Highness was employed, not having as then ye least notice of his march towards Oxford. But before I ingaged myself to stay, I told them I saw in what confusion theire affaires were, whilst noe warrants were observed by ye people, nor directions nor advice for ye welfare of ye towne, any way put into execution.'

Cave immediately wrote to inform the prince of the situation in Hereford and of the imminent arrival of Sir William Waller and of his decision to stay. He also informed Sir William Russell, the Governor of Worcester, of the parlous situation in Hereford, in the hope of some assistance. The scene was set and Cave had now to justify his decision to stay by helping to organise the citizens to mend the defences. It would appear that he put a lot of hope in the use and function of the historic 'Hereford Common Bell.'

The customs, priviledges and boundaries of Hereford had been entered in a book of record at the beginning of the reign of Henry II. Although the original has been lost, Duncumb quoted from a copy that had been translated into English and entitled *A Booke of the priviledges and boundes of the Cittie of Hereford, extracted out of an ancient booke of record.* The part that refers to the common bell reads:

> Concerninge our Bell, wee use that it be in a publique place, where our chief bayliffe [later to become the mayor] may come as well by day as by night, to warne the men inhabiting in the said cittie and suburbs. And wee do not say that it ought to be rung unless it be by reason of ffire ffearfully burning some street of the cittie; or by reason of common mutiny, whereby the cittie might be fearfully troubled; or by reason of some enemies approaching the cittie; or because the cittie is besieged; or some sedition risen among some persons, and made known to the chief bayliffe. And in these cases aforesaid, and all other such like, all within the cittie and suburbs, and within the liberty, at such ringing and moving of the bell, of whatsoever estate they be, ought to come with weapons fitting their estate: and it shall be told them by the chief bayliffe, what is to be done in the behalf of the king, and for the safety and quietness

*The standard of Sir William Waller. A shield hanging from the tree
signifies that glory is the fruit of virtue*

of the cittie. And if any shall refuse to come at the moving of
the bell, let him be accounted for disobedient and perjured.

Sir Richard Cave continued in his testimony to describe the build up to
the attack and his largely unsuccessful attempts to persuade the citizens to
organise themselves and make every attempt to improve the defences of
the city.

Hereupon ye mayor of ye Cittie was instantly sent for, and
desired to summon ye cittizens, to come in with all ye materials
they could bring, to cast up brest-workes to strengthen ye
weakest partes of ye Towne, and upon evry severall place, an
officer of ye ffield was assigned to see it put in execution. This
done, order was given for intelligence ye same evening.

But upon ye next morning, being Monday, not withstanding
the ringing of ye common bell (which is ye strictest summons
that can be given to ye Cittizens, and upon which they are
bound by oath to appear), very few or none came to performe
the intended service; and further upon proclamation, injoyning
them to come in, to worke, upon paine of present plundering,

soe few came in as made not up a worke before one of ye gates above knee high in that whole day; for the other places, which were wholly destitute of any defence, ye officers could not get any to worke.

And although I had severall times before, and once in writing under my hand, given my advice—first, that a breast-worke should be made on ye banke of ye river, upon both sides of ye bridge, and that ye way under ye Castle, being upon ye same banke, very plaine and open as any highway, should be likewise strengthened with a good worke and turnepike, to hinder any entrance by land under ye Castle, or by water in boats;—secondly, that a breast-worke should be cast up to defend ye entrance into ye Castle by ye Mill, as plaine and open a place as the other, only there is a small ascent;—thirdly, that deep trenches, with any moveable bridges, untill draw-bridges could be provided, should be digged and made within every open gate;—fourthly, that Byster's Gate should be dam'd up;—fifthly, that some old houses, in severall places on ye wall should be taken downe: all which workes would have been easily done in twelve houres, by twenty men at a place, save only that worke upon ye bank of ye river, which I conceave would have beene done with much ease by an hundred men in two days; yet none of all these were done, or soe much as offered at, save ye damming up of Byster's Gate, which was done according to my advice.

Besides (which was of more consideration) the stocke of powder was soe short that wee could not discover that there was but five barrells, ye souldiers bandoliers being filled, though ye storekeeper, with ye maior and magistrates of ye towne, were examined before ye Governour, my Lord Scudamore, Colonel Herbert Price and ye reste of ye Councell of Warre; yet since (I know not by what means) more than forty barrells (as I have been credibly informed) have been found by Sir William Waller in ye Towne.

It is evident that the mayor had no intention of helping with the defence of the city and that it was wide open to an attack. Cave, anticipating that the Roundheads would approach from the Ross direction on the eastern bank of the Wye, arranged for Mordiford Bridge to be guarded. He did not anticipate that parliamentary troops, on the western side of the Wye, could cross the river at Hampton Bishop and cut of the guard at the bridge. All the time he was hoping for reinforcements and would have preferred to fight outside the city on a site of his choosing. He went on to write:

But to returne where I left; I spake with Lieut. Col. Courtney on Monday morning, to take speciall care of ye passage of Moorford's Bridge [Mordiford Bridge], where he was quartered, two miles and a half out of Towne, who gave me great incouragement that he could maintaine it, and promised to give a good account thereof. Upon ye other side of ye river there were perpetually scouts abroad to give notice if ye enemy advanced on that side, for my opinion ever was, and I delivered it often, that if any good were done, it must be upon ye way, before he came to ye towne.

On Monday, in ye afternoone, I received Sir William Russel's answere, written the evening before, wherein he gave me first certain notice of Prince Maurice's march towards his Majestie[3]; and that for his owne horse (ye Worcester troop) a great part of them were sent to convey some Scottish Lords, affirming that, untill theire returne, there was noe expectation of any assistance from him; by which wee found wee were to expect neither succour from Worcester, nor diversion from ye Prince.

About ye same time Lieut. Col. Courtney sent for 150 musketiers, advertizing that the enemy was advancing, and within three miles and a halfe of him. Instant orders were given for these musketiers, and they were upon marching, when another messenger from him informed that ye enemy had sent some musketiers before to make good a forde betwixt him and ye towne, and therefore he thought it not safe to stay where he was, but to retreat to ye Towne, which was done accordingly.

Now this forde I never heard of before, being a passe (as I understood afterwards), which might well have been defended, neither could I learne of ye enemy, after he came into ye towne, that he had possessed himself of it with any considerable strength of musketiers.

But I, being a stranger in that countrie, was unaquainted with that and other places of advantage to us, and disadvantage to

3 Royalist forces had been summoned to concentrate at Oxford, leading up to the battle of Newbury.

them. Neither had I time, in that confusion of all things, to informe myselfe by others, having taken upon me to assist those in ye towne but ye very night before.

Lieut. Col. Courtney came not in untill about nine a clocke of ye night, ye horse being soe wearied with continuall duty that some of them lay downe in ye streete, where he made a stand, which nevertheless, considering that ye aforesayd passage was quitted, together with ye weaknesse of ye Towne and magazine, it was my opinion that ye best course was to find out ye enemy in his quarter, or to make ourselves masters of some convenient place neere ye towne before day, where wee might fight with him, or otherwise hinder his passage; and therefore present order was given that the horse should be well fedd, and that both horse and foote should be readie to march by twelve of ye clocke at night.

Instantly after Lieut. Col. Courtney came to my lodging, and there told me that he had 40 or 50 very good men, whose horses were soe beaten out and tired that they would be able to doe very little service, and therefore desired, because his men were very good, and those of ye countie troopes raw, and never upon service, that his better men might mount theire horses, which notion I well liked of, and accordingly order was given.

At midnight, ye time appointed to march, I went into ye Churchyard, where ye foote stood ready; and thence into ye Broad Streete, where ye horse were appointed to be; but finding there not above three or four horses, I was extreamly troubled, and went to ye Lieut. Col.'s lodging, who was abroad calling up his men. Thence I went where ye County troope was quartered, to cause them to make readie theire horses, and then returning to the foote, I marched with them from ye churchyard towards Wigmor's Gate [Widemarsh Gate], thinking that theire moving would be ye only way to draw on ye horse to follow. And coming to ye Market place, I went againe to the Lieut. Col.'s lodging, who was still abroade upon ye same buissnesse. But such was ye indisposition and wearynesse of our men and horse that, in ye space of an hower and an halfe, wee could not bringe above twenty horse together. Soe that wanting horse to doe ye maine intended buissnesse, which was to finde or meete ye enemy, my opinion was to divide those few horse to be imployed upon discovery, one halfe of them one way, and another halfe of them another way. And speciall order was given that ye foote returning to theire severall posts, should stay by theire armes, and the horse should be readie upon any occasion.

Cave's attempts were too late, for the enemy was already within sight of the city. In his testimony he continued to insist that he was not in control of the defenders, but it is evident that he made every effort to defend the city with the meagre forces at his disposal. The attack started:

It was not halfe an hower before one of ye parties of horse returned, and brought word that some of ye enemies muske-tiers were placed in hedges very neere ye towne. Whereupon, on Tuesday morning, ye 25th, I went immediately unto ye Castle (being ye best place to make discovery) where, after a little stay, it beginning to be light, ye enemies whole forces were discov-ered to be within lesse than a mile of ye towne. But ye foote, to whom order was given to stay by theire armes, were most of them gone to theire lodgings, notwithstanding my earnest desire (having noe command over them) that they should stay by theire armes; soe that, considering ye present condition wee were in, I thought it were ye best way to get ye soldiers together at theire severall posts, which was done both by Drum and Trumpet. And whilst they were drawing together, I went from guard to guard to dispose of them to ye best advantage of ye town's defence, forbidding all waste of powder; because ye enemy, approaching nearer and nearer, both in ye ditches and under ye hedges, and in ye suburbs about ye towne, beganne to shoote on all parts.

Thus were lost three severall occasions (for all which it cannot be denyed but that order was given), in ye first place, to take advantage of ye passages; secondly, either to find ye enemy in his quarters, or stop him, and fight with him upon ye way; thirdly, at ye least to draw out before he should enter ye suburbes. None of which it was possible to be done for ye reasons aforesayd. This I am sure, besides these designes of my owne, there was never any motion made by any other for a sallie, either before or after ye enemy came to ye Towne, which I did not most readily embrace and consent to.

My eye was much upon Wigmor's-gate, because I perceaved a body of Horse soe placed as plainly told theire intentions to enter that way; but hearing news that ye enemie were busie about theire boates, I went presently to Wye-bridge, where it was told me that they were carrying over musketiers to ye other side of ye river. Whereupon I sent some of our musketiers from ye Bridge, and a troope of Horse to set upon them, which buissnesse, after some time of dispute, was ended in theire being beaten backe to theire boates. In ye proseqution of this little worke, my Lord Scudamore and ye other Gentlemen present in ye action, can tell how fast powder was consumed, and how quickly; and how many of those which had theire bandiliers full wanted ammunition.

But after ye enemie was thus forced backe, before I could well draw backe over ye bridge, ye horse and musketiers imployed upon this sallie (with some other horse and Dragoones which came to second them), news was brought me that ye enemie was very neere Wigmor's-gate with theire cannon. There was nothing between them and this gate, nor between them and Eyne-gate, but ye plaine streete, with a little iron chayne, knee high, on ye outside, which wee could not hinder them from breaking. I sent present supplies to Wigmor's-gate and then imparted to my Lord Scudamore, Sir William Crofts, Sir Walter Pye, and Col. Herbert Price, what news was brought me, and how much any desperate shotte upon soe weake a gate might indanger ye towne. For our horse were weary and tyred and our foote, though betweene 700 and 800 by list yet were they never upon any service before, so that upon debate wee were put to this choyce, either by sallie to beate the enemie sodenlie from ye towne (for our powder would not last long, and, being spent, we must needs leave both ye towne and ye soldiers to theire mercy), or else to treate, which, for ye present, was judged most usefull, and in a manner necessary, that soe horse and Dragoones, being sent out of towne, might march away securely. And thus it was resolved, and I desired my Lord Scudamore and ye other gentlemen, to go along with them, and leave me there to make ye best conditions I could for ye towne and soldiers, if I should be put to it. At ye first they were resolved to goe, but afterwards they changed that resolution and stayed; and soe Lieut. Col. Courtney marcht away safely with the horse and Dragoones, without any opposition for aught I know, and without ye Gentlemen, who, upon debate, did noe way disapprove of his going.

When wee came to Wigmor's-gate, wee found that ye canon (wherewithall they had severall times shotte through ye gate) did scoure ye streete. Two other passages, one upon and another beneathe ye Castle (both before named), were open for theire entry, for which they were prepared, ye one with boates and ye other by land, nor were they less provided for Eygn-gate.

It is evident that by this time the attacking troops were on the verge of entering the city at several different points. The choice was between house-to-house fighting and surrender. The defenders took the latter course and opened negotiations with Sir William Waller:

Whereupon a parley presently began, which tooke up a greate deale of time before hostages were sent and returned. Those on our side were Sir Walter Pye and Serjeant Major Slaughter; theirs were Lieut. Col. Adams and Serjeant Major Carre. The treatours on our side were Col. Herbert Price and Serjeant Major Dalton; theirs were Col. Carey and (as I remember) a sonne of Sir Robert Cooks, an officer.

The conditions proposed by us were, that if wee were not relieved in four dayes, we would deliver up ye towne, upon condition that wee should march away with flying colours, &c., and that ye church and churchmen, together with ye towne and townsmen, should be free from all violence in their persons and goods; but theire reply was very peremptory and short, demaunding ye towne to be presently rendered to theire commander in chiefe for ye king and parliament, and all ensignes and ammunition of warre, only upon quarter to be given to ye officers and soldiers. Upon ye delivery of which it was received with very much indignation, and for my own particular, I declared that I thought wee ought every man to dy in ye place rather than yield to such conditions. Whereupon Col. James Morgan came from ye place where he stood, and, taking me by ye hand, swore a greate oath he would dy at my foote. I perceaved not any man of another opinion. But then it was mooved that it might bee debated what was fitt to bee done; and it was concluded that ye treatours should goe backe to know if these were ye best condition that they would give us. Upon theire seconde returne, nothing was brought in writing, but ye treatours told us much of theire rigour would bee abated, and thereupon drew up in writing such other articles as they perceaved would bee agreed to, which what they were in particular I cannot possibly remember, only that they were much more reasonable than ye former; but when they went backe with these, ye enemy (saving ye freedome of ye church and towne, in persons and goods) stoode upon as high termes in respect of ye souldiers as before, which was againe generally disliked of. But then, it being againe resumed into debate, severall quere's were made (but none by me) if these demands should not be yielded to, how wee should be able to make our defence, and preserve ye towne; whereunto every man severally replied (not one excepted) that, in his opinion, ye towne (as things then stoode) could not be defended or saved. And I, for my owne part, was of that opinion, though I was none of ye first to declare it. Secondly, it was demanded (since this was the opinion of us all) to what end should wee sacrifice ye souldiers together with ye cittizens, his Majesties good subjects, to ye fury of ye prevailing enemy? Whereunto it was answered and agreed, that rather than doe soe, wee ought to accept of such conditions as were offered, if wee could obtain noe better. Hereupon ye treatours went backe, and ye souldiers and officers, having a hint of this treaty, conveyed themselves out of ye towne with all theire colours, and left not fifty armes behind them, for ought I could learn before coming away from thence. And then ye treatours returned with such articles as engaged us to purchase ye lives of ye souldiers and ye freedome of ye towne, with ye losse of our own liberty. Which articles were first signed by Sir William Waller, and afterwards by ye governor of ye towne, who desired and had of us an acknowledgement under our hands, of our consent to what he had signed.

Hereupon ye enemy enters ye towne, and forthwith ye Lord Scudamore, ye officers, and ye rest of ye Gentlemen, were confined to theire lodgings, from whence ye third night, by ye helpe of ye Alderman's sonne, in whose house I lay, I made my escape over ye towne wall, and through ye mote, which was not over my bootes, intending, as soon as I could, to make my repaire to Oxford; whither I came ye day after, to give an account to his Majestie of ye unfortunate event of this action; and it may bee, I have suffered in ye opinion of ye world, for my open and ingenuous expressions of myselfe.

ARTICLES FOR THE SURRENDER OF THE
CITY OF HEREFORD TO
SIR WILLIAM WALLER
(1643)

1. That the city of Hereford shall bee forthwith surrendered into my hands, for ye service of the King and parliament.

2. That all officers and gentlemen shall have quarter and civill usuage.

3. The ye ordinary souldiers shall have quarter.

4. That all Ladyes and Gentlewomen shall have honourable usage.

5. That ye Armes, Ensignes, and provisions of warre shall bee forthwith surrendered unto mee, or such person or persons as I shall appoint, and that it shall bee free for mee to Quarter in ye citty immediately, with such forces as I shall thinke fitt.

6. That ye Mayor, Aldermen, and Cittizens shall be freed from plunder, and their persons left at liberty for any thing past.

7. That the Bysshopp, and Deane and Chapter, and the collegiates, shall be likewise freed in their persons from violence, and in their goods from plunder.

8. That these Articles bee interchangeably signed by the governour and my selfe.

(Signed)   WILLIAM WALLER

I must not omitte one passage concerning the behaviour of some of ye townsmen toward ye end of ye treaty; for though ye Mayor, with ye chief magistrates and citiizens of ye towne, together with ye clergy, were very well satisfied with ye treaty soe farre as they were concerned in it, yet after it had continued twelve or fourteen howres, some few of them (being of Mr. Coningsby's company) gathered together about Eygngate (I will not say by any man's instigation, though I have beene told soe) and endeavoured to hinder and disturb it, yet soe unreasonably and soe contrary to ye judgement of ye best of ye citie, that ye Governour and Mayor went to ye gate, and, reproving them, made them desist from soe doing.

And now for ye truth of this narrative, I appeale to ye testimonies of ye Lord Scudamore, Sir William Crofts, Sir Walter Pye, and Colonel Herbert Price, who were privy to everything that was done or advised by me. And certainly if I had advised anything to ye prejudice of his Majesties service, or of ye citie and country, men of theire qualitie and known integritie, and soe much interested in ye good of ye place, would have beene soe farre from following my advice, that they would soone have checked and comptrolled me, well knowing I was there upon theire importunity, as an assistant only, without any authority to oblige them to obey mee, as, before I was perswaded to stay with them, I often professed.

Sir Richard Cave made his escape and eventually arrived at Prince Rupert's headquarters where he was arrested. At the time there was another suggestion that the surrender could have been due to the cowardice of the governor, Colonel Herbert Price, but this does not appear from the evidence that Price gave during Cave's Court Martial. Price's evidence was relatively straightforward. During it he explained that 'Waller's forces had shot two pieces of ordnance and divers muskets at the town and soon after generally assaulted it.' He noted especially that Waller had attacked St. Owen's Gate, Widemarsh Gate and the castle. He said that in the opinion of the soldiers the city was not defensible. When asked what forces were there in the city he said: 'about six hundred foot, including three hundred fire-men; and about two hundred and forty townsmen, besides horse and dragoons, amounting to one hundred and eighty.' To the question, 'what was the force of the besiegers?' He replied: 'nineteen companies of dragoons, about thirty companies of horse, and six hundred foot, all fire-men; making in the whole about two thousand five hundred.'

The Court Martial held in Oxford was presided over by Prince Rupert. Richard Cave had to gather together his evidence and wrote specifically to Lord Viscount Scudamore to enlist his help. In that letter he explained that the charge against him was in three parts: that the city of Hereford had been entrusted to him; that he was appointed commander in chief, and that he surrendered it dishonourably.

He said that he had been acquitted on the first two charges, but that on the third charge:

> It is objected that I sent away the Horse and Dragoones (under my particular command) of mine owne head without a Counsell of Warre and without the consent or privitie of any body else, to the great disheartening, weakening and losse of the Towne.
>
> That this was done without a Councell of Warre I have confessed: the Towne then being in that condition that there was noe tyme for a formed Councell of Warre. Witnesse, the Enemyes approach soe near the Towne, that he scoured Wigmore Street with the cannon; and that it did appear to your Lordship and the rest of the Commissioners present with me that the Towne was instantly enterable in diverse places, as is here likewise averred by depositions since. This for the reason of the thing done without a formed Councell of Warre.
>
> That I did it of myselfe, without the consent or privitie of others, I have denyed, as your Lordship knows I have just cause to doe, Your Lordship and other Commissioners being present at the debate of it, and consenting unto it not anyone contra-dicting it. And herein I must entreat your Lordship's particular testimony, to be added to Dr. Sherburne's, who speakes only in the generall; that I sent away the Horse and Dragoones with the consent onely of some few select persons.

He pressed home his case with a series of questions which led to the acceptance of his case; he was freed and every attempt was made to ensure that his reputation was unharmed.

Should there have been any lingering blame attached to this soldier as a result of his actions in Hereford, he amply redeemed it by his gallant death at the Battle of Naseby on 14 June, 1645.

The Judgement of the Court of Warre upon the
Charge laid against
Sir Richard Cave, for the delivery up of
HEREFORD.
OXFORD, 26 Junij, 1643

Whereas Sir Richard Cave hath been accused to His Majesty for the betraying of the Towne of Hereford, when Sir William Waller came before that Towne; and that Accusation was transmitted to the Councell of Warre, whereupon Witnesses were examined upon Oath, and the Court of Warre at severall Dayes heard the Depositions and the whole Cause at large; Upon the full hearing whereof the Court was fully satisfied that Sir Richard Cave was absolutely free from any imputation of any crime to be objected against him for the betraying or delivering up that Towne, or sending away the men under his Command from that Towne at the time when Sir William Waller was before it, and that what he did therein was both by sufficient and full Warrant, and by the advice and consent of the Commissioners of Array for that County who were then present. And this Court hath thought it Just and honourable in them to Declare thus much under their hands, That as farre as in them lyeth they might repare the Reputation of Sir Richard Cave, who hath very unjustly suffered by this Accusation.

RUPERT.	Forth.
Grandison.	Hen: Percy.
Tho: Wentworth	Hen: Wentworth
Joh: Byron	Joh: Belasyse
Will: Pennyman	L: Kirke
Will: Ashbournham	Henry Vaugham

Ro: HEATH present by the Request of the Prince his Highnesse
and the Lord Generall

Directed by the Councell of Warre to be Printed and Published,
and especially to be sent to HEREFORD

CHAPTER SIX

After the Surrender

Although Sir William Waller had achieved a momentous victory by forcing Hereford to yield within less than a day (as a result Waller became known as William the Conquerer), he was not in a position to hold it for any length of time. Indeed, within a fortnight of the surrender, there were no Parliamentarians left in Hereford.

Apart from the direct results of plundering in the city and neighbourhood and cash gleaned from anxious citizens attempting to preserve their houses and property, Waller's most significant reward was some two dozen prisoners, all 'men of note, quality and good estate.' They included: Sir Richard Cave, who succeeded in escaping three days later; Colonel Herbert Price, the governor of the city and M.P. for Brecon; Fitzwilliam Coningsby of Hampton Court, the High Sheriff of the county; Lord Viscount Scudamore of Holme Lacy, probably the most important of the prisoners; Sir William Croft of Croft Castle, M.P. for Malmesbury, he was slain whilst fighting for the king at Stokesay Castle on 8 June, 1645; Sir Walter Pye of the Mynde and owner of Kilpeck Castle, the son of the king's late Attorney General; James Scudamore Esq., M.P. for Hereford; Humphrey Coningsby of Hampton Court; Lieutenant-Colonel Courteney, who had been in charge at Mordiford Bridge and acted as second-in-command to Sir Richard Cave; Sir Samuel Aubrey of Clehonger; Colonel James Morgan; Dr. Rogers[1]; two Drs. Goodwin and Dr. Evans, all of the

---

1 Dr Henry Rogers was Canon Residentiary of Hereford Cathedral and Rector of Stoke Edith. He was a noted Royalist and famous preacher. Eventually his prebendal house together with all the furniture was sequestered and bestowed on Dr. Timothy Woodroffe who was a parliamentary preacher in the cathedral, having been promoted to the rectory of Kingsland by Sir Robert Harley.

cathedral; Lt-Col. Thomas Price; Sgt. Major Minbridge (who was badly injured); Sgt. Major Slaughter; Sgt. Major Dalton and Captains Somerset and Sclater.

These and several others were sent to Gloucester where they stayed for a short while before being moved to Bristol. Although there were some threats against them during their imprisonment, they were eventually liberated on the last day of June, 1643, when Bristol surrendered to Prince Rupert. They returned to Herefordshire full of zeal and determined to ensure that the city did not fall again to the parliamentarian forces. The mayor, William Price, apparently came in for some harsh treatment. His house and shop were plundered, he was called a rebel and traitor, and threats were made to hang him at his front door. Was it as a result of this rough usage that he died in 1643? Thomas Rogers was elected in his place, but he also died, having been in office for only a short time. Rogers was followed by Philip Trahearne, the third mayor of Hereford in 1643.

One of the prisoners was not taken to Gloucester. This was Viscount Scudamore of Holme Lacy. Born in 1600, he was elected to Parliament for Herefordshire in 1620 and for Hereford City in 1625. On 1 July, 1628, he was created Baron Dromore and Viscount Scudamore of Sligo. He was a friend and admirer of Archbishop Laud and amongst other religious works carried out major repairs to Dore Abbey. Following his appointment by Charles I as Ambassador to Louis XIII in 1634, he spent several years in France. He returned to Holme Lacy in January, 1639, and was immediately made Chief Steward of the city. For some time before the war started he had been busy collecting together a vast collection of weapons at Holme Lacy to arm his followers.

He was considered one of the most important and prestigous of the prisoners taken by Waller and was afforded special treatment. A few days after the surrender, he was informed that he must appear before Parliament in London. A pass was made out to allow him to travel through the areas controlled by the parliamentarian troops:

> These are to will and require all souldiers to permit the Lord Scudamore with his traine, to passe thiere guards; and for thiere soe doing this shall be theire warrant. Given under my hand, at Hereford, this 29th April, 1643.
>
> WILLIAM WALLER.

Scudamore arrived in London on 13 May, 1643, and went to his town house in Petty France. (This house adjoined that in which Milton, a friend

John, First Viscount Scudamore

of Scudamore, subsequently wrote *Paradise Lost.*) It is apparent that he felt
that his treatment at the hands of Sir William Waller had been quite
reasonable. The following day he wrote to Sir Robert Pye, the uncle of the
Sir Walter Pye who had been involved in the siege of Hereford, as follows[2]:

> SIR, — It was my fortune to bee in Hereford when Sir William
> Waller took it. And being a person that abounds in civilitie, hee
> did me the honour to come to mee to the place where I lodged,
> and, after some passages of noble respect, hee desired mee to

2 Sir Robert Pye, the Auditor of Receipt of the Exchequer, was an ardent Royalist
and garrisoned his mansion at Faringdon, in Berkshire, for the king. There, he was
besieged by his eldest son, also Robert, who was a colonel of cavalry under Fairfax,
and son-in-law of John Hampden.

consider him as the centurion's servant who was to doe as hee was commanded, that hee was governed by instructions, and according unto them was to intreat mee to apply myself, in what convenience I might, to goe to London to the Parliament. The answere I made him was, that I should be ready to obey his commandments. And speaking to him concerning the way and time of me going up, hee was pleased to leave me to myself to goe how I would, and to take my word that I would bee heere by last night.

After this I waited upon him at his quarter, and carrying with mee a copy of the Treaty upon which the Town was surrendered, I observed unto him, that by the sixt Article of the Treaty, I conceaved both my person and goods to bee free for anything past, as being a citizen and having had the happiness long since to serve under that quality, as an unworthy member of the honourable house of Commons. And, therefore, I desired that I might enjoy the justice and benefitt of that Article, and if there were no other reason than my being in Hereford when the town was rendered up, I presumed it was in his power to excuse mee from the journey to London. Hee made answere, that hee had already written up how that hee found mee in Hereford, and that I would bee shortly in London, and that hee had taken my word for it; and that besides hee had represented how much I had suffered, and how little I had acted, and that having gone thus farre it would bee not decent for him to thinke upon freeing mee in the country, but that hee did not doubt but I should find so easy a passage in the Parliament as would bee even beyond my expectation. Whereupon I continued my self to my former engagement, and am accordingly come hither. It was yesterday in the evening before I arrived heere, so that I can not make offer of my self to the Parliament till tomorrow morning that they sitt. But then my request, Sir, to you is, that you will favour me so much as to acquaint the honourable house of Commons, both with the contents of this my letter, and that I am arrived and doe attend heer with all humbleness, to receive and submitt unto their pleasure and commaunds.

Being come, I find the house I lived in lately, in Petty France and the goods in it are nearly sequestered upon a general ordinance of Parliament. I trust and humbly move, that since I have brought my person hither, the House will be pleased to give order that this sequestration may bee taken off, or otherwise to refer it to a committee. And I hope further, that when a thorough search shall have been made of mee it will be found that neither bitterness of mind against persons, nor greedy desire of any worldly thing, have moved mee to or fro in the carriage of my self amidst these dismall distractions and divine judgements upon my deare mother England, but that I have desired and laboured to keep a good conscience, according to the best of my understanding; and though it should proove to bee an erring conscience, yet it had been sinne in mee to goe against it, being mine. So, Sir, I take leave and rest,

Your affectionate friende,

To serve you,

PETTY FRANCE, May 14, 1643.   SCUDAMORE

A few days later Scudamore wrote a second letter to Pye, offering to ransom himself and providing Pye, and through him the House of Commons, with details of the damage he had sustained at his houses at Holme Lacy in Herefordshire, at Llanthony House in Gloucestershire, and in London. He provides a vivid picture of the extent of general plundering and malicious damage that was occurring throughout the country as the various warring armies took whatever they wanted from wherever they could find it.

SIR,— I humbly desireth to redeem my liberty with a summe of money, and do conceive that the honourable house of Commons will not onely incline to suffer mee to receive this favour which they graunt to many, but will also use mee without rigour in the proportion of the mulct, the rather in regard my sufferings have been already great, and my doings onely such as have expressed consiencenous of duty according to my understanding without bitterness of mind towards persons or sinister designs upon things.

My sufferings consist much in these following particulars. My armes were taken away from my house in Herefordshire. Divers of my goodes and hangings and carpetts and my wive's apparell have been seisd on in London and carried to the Guild Hall. Two Houses of mine by Gloster are defaced and the one of them so that it goes beyond the extremity used to the house of any person that hath been declard the greatest adversary of

Parliament (unless such have been burned or pulled down). First the hangings, linen, pewter, brass and all moveables carried away. Then the glass of the windows all broken; the barrs of the windows, locks, bolts, hinges of doors carried away, the ceilings broken down, the flooring of boards broken up and burnt or sold, nay the very stayres taken down and burnt together with the vessells which after the Beer was drunk up were thrown into the fire, though there were wood and cole in good plenty. In fine not so much as a beame left in the house onely the rafters remaine which hold up the tiles. I particularise it thus to shew the malice that accompanied this carnage, and so the abuse of the Parliament's authority wunder the colour whereof this is done, and so the greater affliction upon mee.

My other house there they have taken the lead of it which covered it, pulld down two corners of it, and cutt down many trees which were not onely an ornament but a necessary shelter from the violences of Winter and Summer. Besides, all the trees (are) fallen between Lanthony-House and Gloster. And for addition to these losses it is reported that the whole rent of that estate is seisd on by demand of some at Gloster under colour of authority of Parliament. Besides my wife was restrained of her liberty without cause, much frighted by souldiers, and although sickly and unfitt for travell, was forced to deliver herself by a hard adventure of a night journey at Christmas, behind one of horseback. I hear of few women so used with these troubles.

These are the suffrings layd upon mee. I leave my doings to be sett forth by my greatest enemies, desiring onely they may not bee believed without proofe. And then I persuade my selfe every unpartiall eye, comparing both together, will thinke my suffrings already have been so much above the proportion of my desert, that there will remaine very little in reason to bee added for this action of Hereford, wherein I was but a volunteer, and had no command, and being heer casually and a sworn citizen and steward of the town, I knew not how in honour to run away from it, just when a force appeared before it.

(signed) SCUDAMORE

He was totally unsuccessful with his plea, to the extent that a couple of weeks later on Monday, 29 May, 1643, it was 'Ordered by the Commons assembled in parliament that the goods seized of the Lord Scudamores bee forthwith solde and the proceeds thereof employed for the service of the forces under the Command of Sir Wm. Waller.' The entire property was sold to one Thomas Vyner, a goldsmith of London for £176 15s.

Meanwhile, in Herefordshire, Lady Scudamore was approaching the problems of damage to their property in Gloucester from a different direction. She was still at Holme Lacy while her husband was under arrest in London. She wrote to Sir William Waller, who had also returned to Gloucester, complaining about the treatment she had received and obviously had more success than her husband in preserving their homes and valuables, for in his reply the ever courteous Waller wrote:

> Noble lady
> I shall ever take itt as a great honour to receive your commands, and I shall, with a ready obedience, entertaine them.
> In obedience to your ladyshipps letter, I sent for Alderman Pury, and questioned with him what wast had been committed on your ladyshipps house or grounds. I finde some trees have been felled, and have given order, there shall be no more touched; but I am assured nothing about the house hath been defaced, only a tower of an old chappel adjoyning thereunto was pulled down, in regard itt might have been some annoyance to the workes. For your ladyshipps rents I have given order the sequestration should not bee executed; so that, Madam, they are still at your command. If there be anything else wherein I may advance your ladyshipps service, I humbly beg the favour to be commanded, that I may have opportunity to give some demonstration with what passion
> I am, Madam, Your devoted humble servant
Waller
>
> Gloucester, June 4, 1643

Lord Scudamore was unfortunate, not only because of his tremendous losses, estimated to be £37,690, but also because he was held captive for at least another two years ten months (some authorities say three-and-a-half years) before purchasing his release for the sum of £2,690.

During his later years Scudamore devoted himself to the study of history and theology and to the care and relief of impoverished clergy. He is perhaps best remembered for his research on grafting and planting apple orchards. He was responsible for the redstreak apple used for many years in cider production, as recorded in Philips's *Cyder.*

Of no regard till Scudamore's skilful hand
Improv'd her, and by courtly discipline
Taught her the savage nature to forget,—
Hence styl'd the Scudamorean plant.

As for the other prisoners, they were released when Bristol surrendered to Prince Rupert at the end of June, 1643, and returned to Hereford pondering how they could advance the king's interests in their home county.

There was still one area of Herefordshire where parliamentary rule was accepted—the few villages in the extreme north-western corner where Sir Robert Harley held sway. All were within the protection of the ancient castle of Brampton Bryan. Sir Robert continued to take an active part in parliamentary activities, leaving no doubt where his interests lay, whilst his wife, Brilliana, was entrusted with the custody of the castle. The reduction of this stronghold was an object dear to the heart of all Herefordshire Royalists, and on 26 July, Sir William Vavasour, then Governor of Hereford, with some 600 men, laid siege to the castle, a siege that continued for a month.

On 25 August, Brilliana wrote to her son, 'My deare Ned, the gentillmen of the cuntry have affected theair desires in bringing an army against me. What spoyls has bine doun, this barer will tell you. Sir William Vavasor has left Mr. Lingen with the soulders. The Lord in mercy presarve me.'

A few days later her wishes were granted. Henry Lingen, on hearing that the king had been defeated at Gloucester, withdrew on 6 September to go to his assistance. The church and village had been burnt during the siege, but at the castle a troop of 600 men had been successfully repelled for a full six weeks by a small band of puritan ministers, retainers and domestic servants led by an old soldier from the German wars called Hackluit, and strongly supported by the mistress of the house. Lady Brilliana had been ill for several years and the siege must have been the final blow to her delicate health. On 9 October she wrote to her son, 'I have taken a very greate coold, which has made me very ill these 2 or 3 days.' She died a day later within the walls of the house she had so well defended.

Brampton Bryan Castle survived a little longer, but was again besieged in March, 1644. Cannon was brought against it and eventually the defenders had to surrender. A contemporary account describes the walls as being 'battered even with the ground leaving little else but the cellars'. The direct losses of Sir Robert Harley in building and furnishings was £6,650 including a study of books and invaluable historical documents valued at £200.

The ruins of Brampton Bryan Castle as depicted by the Buck brothers in 1731

Problems also weighed on the mind of Joyce Jefferies. She stayed at Garnons throughout the whole of 1643, but from time to time made arrangements to cover her responsibilities in the city:

1643 July 4 Paid to a man for watching a night at
Widemarsh gate   4d.
Oct.   Rece. of Leifftenant Rogers (that cam out of
Ireland with a troop of souldiers to Leominster
for the king) for my gray nagge   £4 5s.
Nov 24 Gave a poore souldier to help to heale his head
6d.
Paid a lewne in Heriford towards the fier at the
gates in heriford for ye sowldiers to watch bye
4s.

It was Easter, 1644, when she returned to Hereford to settle her affairs and then stay at with her cousin at Homcastle at Clifton-on-Teme. She handed out favours to the servants at Garnons and her steward, Mathais Rufford, arranged for her belongings to be moved from Garnons to Homcastle.

1644 April 17 This day I cam from Garnons to heriford ... to
my owne howse
On Shrove Tuesday, at heriford, to John
Cappe, alias Stefens, for cariing some clothes
of myne from Garnons to Heriford   6d.
April 19 I cam from Heriford to Homcastle on
Good Friday, 1644

She continued to have responsibilities in Hereford and whilst she was prepared to pay, she objected to her goods being sequestered.

1644 May Gave an honest carpinder for preserving my
tymber from the Governors knowledge, which
sought for tymber to make works to defend
heriford   1s.
Paid for work donn in making bullwarks to
defend the Citty of heriford from invasion 20d.

By this time Hereford was effectively under military law, the Governor being Colonel Nicholas Mynne. However, he, together with much of his

Anglo-Irish regiment, was killed at a particularly bloody action at Redmarley, in Gloucestershire, in August, 1644.

Mrs. Jefferies continued to receive rents from her properties in Hereford but decided not to continue with her rented house:

> 1644   Aug   Paid to workmen for cariinge som houshold [goods] from my lower Howse in Heriford to my upper new howse in ye same Widmarsh streete
>
> 11s.
>
> October   Paid Mrs Fletcher and her mother-in-law one yeares rent for the ould house I did dwell in Widmarsh streete in heriford, due at Micklmas, 1644; then I left ye howse   £6

For over a year, Hereford had been peaceful and she must have felt that by this time her other property in Hereford was reasonably secure for:

> 1644   August   Gave Mr. Dockter Aldern's man for his horses to fetch my coach from Garnons to heriford   1s.

Her optimism, as far as her property was concerned, was not justified, for she had not bargained for the activities of the man who was to become the new Governor of Hereford, Colonel Barnabas Scudamore.

Although Hereford remained in Royalist hands for over two years after Waller abandoned the city, tension still remained high, with due cause. About the middle of April, 1644, the parliamentarian commander, Massey, with 400 foot, and Purefoy, with a regiment of horse, left Gloucester and took up quarters at Ledbury. Throughout the area they made assessments and collected as much money as possible. After a few days they made a reconnaissance in some force westwards as far as Hereford. The whole of the horse and some 150 musketeers arrived outside the city and made every effort to provoke the defenders by firing a house in the suburbs, but no-one ventured outside the walls.

It is evident that the parliamentary troops were looking for mischief and, on the way back to Ledbury, they stopped at Stoke Edith. This was the home of the well-known Royalist, Henry Lingen, whilst the rector was Henry Rogers D.D., well known as a 'pestilent preacher against the Parliament.' It was here, by St. Edith's Well, that the troops came across John Pralph, the aged vicar of Tarrington, who was on his way home from Hereford. His venerable appearance (he was some 80 years old) would at one time have secured him respect and, even then, should have protected him from aggression. However, it was not to be, for he was given the standard challenge 'Who are you for?' The standard answer was 'for the King and Parliament', but the old gentleman had spirit and replied 'for God and the King.' Immediately 'the barbarous Rebell shot him through the head with his Pistoll.' The Tarrington Parish register records 'May 3— 1644. Burial. John Pralph, Vicar. He was murdered by some of the Parliament Soldiers near the Well at Stoke Edith.'

It would not have been long before the news of Colonel Massey's attempt on Hereford reached the king. He responded on 8 May by issuing instructions that Hereford should be fortified and placed under a governor. Massey continued with his minor actions in the area as part of his efforts to gain the initiative in Herefordshire and Gloucestershire. He occupied Ross for a short time in May, whilst he assessed and collected levies, and followed it with the occupation of Tewkesbury.

By June, the Royalists were having difficulty in recruiting men and the king gave full authority to the governors of Hereford and Worcester to impress men and horses for their regiments, to assess and levy contributions for their payment, to billet and quarter their men as required and to seize all arms. In effect martial law had been declared and the governor had the power to do anything that might advance the king's cause. Sir William Vavasour, who had laid siege to Brampton Bryan the previous year was described as the 'Governor of this Cittie' in August, 1643, but had apparently been replaced by Colonel Nicholas Mynne by the following May. Mynne was killed at the skirmish at Redmarley in August, 1644, and was replaced as governor of Hereford for a short while by a Colonel Barnard. He was superseded on 10 September by an officer well known in Herefordshire, Colonel Barnabas Scudamore.

When Scudamore took over the governorship of the city, he carried out a careful check on the accounts and established that the total amount raised from assessments and loans from the departure of Vavasour to 14 September, 1644, amounted to £2,438 15s. $7^{1}/_{2}$d, the disbursements being some two pounds less. On that day there were in the city 466 men in arms of all grades, the weekly cost being £53 4s. Although there is no indication whether they were trained soldiers or 'volunteers', they were probably foot soldiers. It is apparent that they were lodged in houses throughout the city, and that they had a weekly allowance of rye in addition to their pay. The following list gives an indication of the billeting in the various city wards:

Charles R

Most deare & entirely beloved Nephew Wee greete you well.
The Committee of the Lords & Comons here assembled apprehending
the danger that Our Citty of Hereford is subiect vnto by the
frequent Incursions of the Rebels into those parts, haue
desired Us that the said Citty may be forthwith fortify'd at
y[e] charge of that Citty & County, and that there may be a
Gouernor appointed to reside constantly there to take care
for the defence thereof; W[i]ch desires of the said Comittee
Wee haue thought good by these Our Letters earnestly to
recomend to you to be speedily ordered & provided for in such
manner as you shall conceive most for the Securrity of
the said Citty & County, & the most good to Our Seruice.
And soe Wee bid you most heartily farewell. Giuen at
Our Court at Oxford the 8[th] day of May 1644.

By his Ma[tie]s Comand

Edw: Nicholas

Charles's letter issuing instructions for the fortification of Hereford
and for the appointing of a governor

Anno Dm 1644:
September the 09th delivered unto the
Inhabitants of the Cittie of Heref:
where the souldiers are billetted as
followeth

Wyebridge Warde	103 Souldiers quartered: at 3 pecks a peece	309
Eigne Warde	104 Souldiers quartered: at 3 pecks Rye	312
Widmarsh Warde	052 Souldiers quartered: at 3 pecks Rye	156
Bisters Warde	116 Souldiers quartered: at 3 pecks Rye	348
St. Owens Warde	<u>033</u> Souldiers quartered: at 3 pecks Rye	<u>099</u>
	408	1224

Maketh bushells 306

At a slightly later date several were billeted with Mrs. Jefferies:

1645   March   Gave to souldeers that were sent to be quartered in my new house 3 severall tymes   16d

The country was full of action throughout the summer of 1644. The king travelled from Oxford to Worcester and then to Bewdley, pursued by Sir William Waller. They met at Cropredy Bridge near Banbury on 28 June where the king gained the advantage. The royal army moved to Evesham for a short while and then, in the middle of July, marched into the West Country where they were successful in routing Essex's army. The king eventually returned to the Midlands to raise the siege of Banbury and then retired to Oxford for the winter.

Late in 1644, Cromwell came to the fore and early the following year he managed to persuade Parliament that Members should resign their military commands (the Self-Denying Ordinance) and that the various parliamentary armies should be amalgamated under a single command. The result, the New Model Army under the command of Sir Thomas Fairfax, was an efficient, fully mobile army under the control of proficient and dedicated officers.

The first great test of this New Model Army came in June, 1645. The Royalist army, under the leadership of Prince Rupert, had successfully attacked Leicester during the previous month. Fairfax moved his new army against Rupert's forces and they met at the Battle of Naseby in Northamptonshire on 14 June, 1645. The New Model Army together with Cromwell and his cavalry was more than a match for the small Royalist army and Rupert's forces were routed, loosing much of their baggage. The king retreated westwards and passed through Kidderminster, Bewdley and Bromyard on the way to his destination, Hereford, where he arrived on Thursday,19 June. Charles had travelled some 120 miles in only five days to arrive at a safe haven and stayed in the city for almost a fortnight.

In Hereford, he wrote to the Earl of Glamorgan: 'As my selfe is nowais dishartned by our late misfortune so nether this Country, for I could not have expected more from them, than they have now freely undertaken, though I had come hither absolute Victorius, which makes me hope well of the nighboring Sheeres; so that (by the grace of God) I hope shortly to recover my late losse, with advantage, if such succours come to me, from that Kingdome, which I have reason to expect.' On the same day he wrote to his son, the Prince of Wales, and discussed the possibility of his own capture.

Whilst the king was still lodging in Hereford, Scudamore wrote to all the parishes in the county in an attempt to raise new forces for the Royalist army. To the parish of Clifford he wrote:

By his Majesties express Command at the unanimous desier of the Gentry and other Inhabitants of this County assembled the 21st of June at Hereford I am to Require you Mr Thomas Penoyer and Mr John Higgins gent. to cause forthwith to be listed within the parish of Clifford, thirty seaven able bodied men such as you shall judge fittest for Service, and to cause them without fayle to appeare at the gen'all Rendezvous at Wigmarsh the 28 day of this month, and to cause a months contribucon of your parish to be collected and brought in by you at the same time for the providing of Muskets Bandileers &c for the sayd Soldiers so brought in. And you are likewise Required to cause one list of the sayd persons so brought in and their habitacons to be kept in the Constables hands of the parish and another of the same to be returned to the Comissioners that a fittinge course may be taken with those that shall happen to Runne away, according to a proclamation to be yssued for that purpose. And that all the Constables and other officers and inhabitance are to be aydinge and assistinge unto you as they will answere the contrary at their perills.
B. Scudamore
Hereff the 22nd of June 1645

Even with such threats, the king's attempts to obtain new recruits to his cause apparently had little success. However, it appears that he was more successful in obtaining financial contributions collecting some £5,000 from the county. The king left Hereford on 1 July and was accompanied towards Abergavenny by, amongst others, Henry Lingen and Barnabas Scudamore. It was during this march, at a remote house near Grosmont, that Lingen received the honour of knighthood.

Afterwards, Scudamore issued his 'Warrant for the Apprehension of Deserters'. This was not just an attempt to gather in those who had deserted, but was an attempt to persuade the parishes to provide their quota of men. His final threat was of somewhat doubtful force: 'if you faile in either I ame by his Majesties Command to Returne unto hime your persones to bee disposed of according to his Majesties Plesure.'

Barnabas Scudamore, then about 36 years of age, was the only surviving brother of John, Lord Scudamore, who was still a parliamentary prisoner. He had been involved with the king in the Scottish battles and had later been wounded. As a soldier with reasonable experience of warfare and a well-known member of the gentry in Herefordshire, he was probably a good choice as governor of the city, although he would have to make several unpopular decisions.

One of his first problems was the arrival on the scene of a third force— the Clubmen. This rather nebulous force consisted of a banding together of farmers and peasants into a loose society to 'redress the fruits of the civil war' including 'robberies, ravashings and innumerable wicked actions, committed by barbarous soldiers.' Although the Clubmen professed neutrality it was the Royalists in Shropshire who first bore the brunt of this force who were 'neither for King nor Parliament, but stand on their own guard for the preservation of their lives and fortunes.' From Shropshire, the movement spread into Worcestershire and 'by degrees the cloud had rolled on towards Herefordshire, and burst on a sudden with violence and disorder. Oppression was their pleas: neutrality their cry.'

By March, 1645, the situation had reached slightly more serious proportions and Scudamore had to send out troops to Broxash Hundred where there was an affray. Scudamore, with more important things on his mind, is reputed to have declared that he would 'hang the dogs and drown their whelps,' but when some 15,000 to 16,000 Clubmen (including contingents from Worcestershire and Radnorshire) presented themselves in front of the walls of Hereford on 19 March, he realised that a more conciliatory course of action was needed. The Clubmen presented their demands, which included the 'withdrawal of the garrison of Canon Frome' (there were apparently Irish troops here who were particularly brutal in their oppression of the countryside) and that 'such as were held prisoners there, should be delivered forthwith; that satisfaction should be given to the country for the losse they sustained by plunder, as also to the wives and children of those that were slaine, that the country might be freed from contribution ...' They also wanted to take over the garrisoning of Hereford which, they insisted, they could do better and thus defend the whole county.

Scudamore replied with a manifesto that recognised their 'just grievances' and promised to 'protect them with all the strength under my command.' He was prepared to forget all that was past upon 'their submission and protestation to pay Contribucions and in all other thinges faithfully to serve his Majestie.' Scudamore managed to make a peace with the rebels just before the princes Rupert and Maurice arrived in the area having heard of the problems. A few Clubmen demonstrated against the princes' troops near Ledbury, but they were disarmed, their leaders taken and three of them hanged. The Clubmen had achieved a few minor promises, but Prince Rupert rapidly made sure there was no re-occurrence by ensuring that the appropriate dues were collected immediately and that every person in 'every town, parish and village' in Worcestershire and Herefordshire should take a loyal oath to the king on pain of imprisonment.

Hereford had been taken twice by parliamentarian forces and Scudamore was determined to make sure that it did not happen again. He had several advantages, for the city was under military rule and a fund had been established by assessments and loans to repair and improve the defences. His achievements were considerable and it is apparent that he carried out much of the work recommended by Sir Richard Cave in advance of Sir William Waller's attack, but not implemented. He must have strengthened all the gates, presumably with new timber doors, and replaced any fixed bridges with drawbridges. He would also have carried out some repair work at the castle, but his main effort was to clear the areas outside the gates. The buildings that had gradually grown outside the gates were obviously of greater benefit to the attackers than the defenders and, to provide clear fields of fire from the gates and walls, they had to be demolished. Sir Henry Slingsby, a noted Royalist officer, remarked on the devastation:

Here we found all places about ye town made Levell, where as before they stood upon ye same ground, fair houses and Goodly Orchards. I went to see ye house where I formerly Quartered, &

Prince Rupert, by Gerard Honthorst

found it pull'd down, & ye Gentlewoman yt lived in it dead upon grief to see ye ruins of her house.

Mrs. Jefferies was made of sterner stuff and just entered in her accounts:

| 1645 | May | Rece. of Maud Prichet half a yeers rent for her howse in Widmarsh streete in Heriford, due at Holirood day, 1645, being the last that ever she paid, for she removed, and my howses were pulled downe | 30s. |

Indeed, she had little choice for she entered:

1645	June	The severall names of those men that bought my 3 houses in Heriford without widmarsh gate, when I was constraind to sell them or have them burned	
	Imp.	young Mr holmes the mercer in heriford bought my greate new howse (hit stood me in above £500) with a greate deale of squared tymber at the saw pitt, with glasse: and all apurtinances ther to	£50
	It.	Haiward a tailer, and William Price shue maker, Bought my howse over the way called Gowlding Halle for	£3.15s.
		Phillip Preece Bought Maud Pritchet's Halle and the inner Roome	£4
		Walter Merrick and on Butler bought the great Hale, and the rooms over hit.	£11
		Joseph Bowker Bought the Roomes over the Staiers case by the well at	£3

Thus in total she received £71 15s. for all her property outside Widemarsh Gate. She tried to retrieve as much as possible and sent her steward, Mathais Rufford, to look after her interests in the city. He was presumably there just before the Scots army appeared at the end of July:

1645	July	Paid Mathais Rufford diet and a horse 8 daies in heriford being there to poole downe ye glasse in ye windose, and the dores, and in going Abroad: both in ye Cittye and County upon my busines, at 1s. a day, with garden Salitts	8s.
		Paid the glazier for pulling down the glass	18d.
		Paid him for cariing hit and putting hit into the two greate chests in ye gardin	8d.

Gave John Joiner for helping to cary in the
dores, shelfes, and wainscott, out of the saw
pitt in my new gardin, into my coache howse

6d.

The glass was of considerable value and must have been buried in the garden for, once the siege was safely over there is an entry:

1646 Jan. 17   Gave David Williams, ye bailiff at Homcastle, for
helping to gett my truncks out of ye ground

6d.

CHAPTER SEVEN

The Scots army arrives

Late in 1643, well before Cromwell formed the New Model Army, Parliament secured the services of the Scots army to fight their battles for them, partly by promises of pay and partly by agreeing to the Solemn League and Covenant which allowed the Scots religious conformity based on Scottish Presbyterianism. This army significantly altered the balance of power away from the king and in favour of Parliament.

The Scots army was under the control of Alexander Leslie, First Earl of Leven. He was born about 1580 and was approaching 65 when he commanded the siege of Hereford. He was one of the most experienced generals of the age, having served in the army of the Swedish king for over thirty years. He was in sympathy with the Scottish Covenanters and returned to Scotland to lead the army in 1638. He continued in charge of Scotland's armies until well into the 1650s, dying on his estate in Fifeshire in 1661.

This new force entered England early in 1644 and headed towards York, which was already under siege. They invested it for nine or ten weeks before Prince Rupert came to its relief from his base at Shrewsbury. This led to the Battle of Marston Moor on 2 July. Initially, the parliamentary army, under the control of Lord Leven and Lord Fairfax, was in utter confusion following a brilliant attack by Rupert's cavalry, and Leven had to flee the field together with some of his army. The first news that arrived in Hereford related to this trouncing and at All Saints Church on 8 July Royalist sentiments came to the fore when:

It paid for wringing at the Scots overthrow in the Northe
By Mr. Maiors apointment   2s. 6d.

The bells must have been rapidly muted when the full news of the battle was heard. For the situation at Marston Moor rapidly changed when Leven's lieutenant and relative, David Leslie, together with Cromwell, stood their ground and won the day. In the bloodiest battle of the Civil War, the king's northern army was routed with the loss of over 4,000 dead and of control over much of the north country. Leven returned to be present at the surrender of York on 16 July and went on to take Newcastle. In early in 1645 he moved into Westmorland and thence south.

The army consisted of 8,000 foot under the Earl of Leven, and about 4,000 horse led by Sir David Leslie and Colonel Middleton. Some had seen service in Ireland and others in the low countries. Various descriptions of the Scots army were published—the following are a sample from both sides. A testimonial, self-produced by the Scots Army, was published in *The Scotch Intelligencer*, 19 to 25 Oct, 1643:

> The Scottish army hath a very able traine of artillerie, and many pretty engines for war, and devises for killing Cavaliers and Papists; the noble and able general Lisly [Lesley] hath contrived these, and many other excellent utinsells for War.
>
> They are setting out orders of discipline for the Army, which will be very strict and severe, for it is one of our best principles to keepe our souldiers at command; and I dare say a proud word, never was a better disciplined Army in the Christian world than ours. We have no dangerous mutinies, nor repinings, nor complaints, but an universall cheerfulness in our whole body. You will not believe how peacibly we marched with our Army when we came last into England, and how we kept them in order; never did Army make less spoile, commit less violence, fewer plunderings, unless he were a bad man indeede and a very enemy to the cause, and then we borrowed something of him till our returne.
>
> Our Army is very hardy too, and can endure all heates and colds, and a small victailing will serve the turne; a little paste well kneaded in the palme of their hands is there usuall dyet, and they are not so tender as your English Cavaliers, who love ease, and eating, and carousing. They will find wee are to hard for them in our marchings; wee never scruple att winter nor bad weather, if the way will but fit for the carriage of ordnance we shall travail ourselves well enough; we can trott over the mountaines and forrests of snow when the Cavaliers sett down over a fire.

Alexander Leslie, Earl of Leven, by Jamesone

This description should be compared with those of other writers that are, perhaps, a little nearer to the truth. One such stated that:

> The Scots marched with a very sorry equipage; every soldier carried a week's provision of oatmeal, and they had a drove of cattel with them for their food. They had also an invention of guns of white iron, tinned and done about with leather, and chorded so that they could serve for two or three discharges. These were light, and were carried on horses.

A more amusing description was included in several of the journals that were being published in increasing numbers to satisfy peoples' needs for hard news of the war:

> There is likewise providing for our army [of] 5,000 Redshanks or Highlanders. These are not so civilized as we could wish, but they are good soldiers and hardy men, and are usually clad in a light plaid or speckled stuff; and in this attire they usually march, never using any armes upon their bodies. They have darts, and bows and arrowes, and durkes or great knives; and which is a wonder (for they are none of them very religious) yet they all hate bishops, papists, and caviliers, and they threaten to pull them all to pieces, one limne from another. They are mad to heare how they abuse their king, and these do wonderfully love your parliament, and vow to venture all the blood under their plaid for the good Lords and Gentiles of your parliament, especially your House of Commons; and they say that they have no such skill of your lords, yet we persuade them to think well of your lords too, and tell them how all the rotten peares are dropt off, and that now they are a bonny company, and may do muche good for God and their country.

Despite all the promises, these men were paid only sporadically and regularly complained about the lack of any provision of food. It would appear that on the march and during the siege of Hereford they relied almost entirely on raw pears, apples and green corn. This could well have been one of the main reasons for their sickness, mortality and lack of spirit. Even so, they ravaged the land and took all they could lay their hands on and, in addition, imposed large sums on all the towns and villages through which they passed.

Parliament had allotted £21,000 per month to pay the troops. The rates were fixed:

Horse:

Major of horse	6s. 0d.
Captain of horse	6s. 0d.
Lieutenant of horse	4s. 0d.
Cornet	2s. 6d.
Corporal or Trumpeter	1s. 6d.
Trooper (for his diet)	1s. 0d.

The foot soldiers received less:

Major of foot	4s. 0d.
Captain	3s. 0d.
Lieutenant	2s. 0d.
Ensign	1s. 6d.
Sergeant	1s. 0d.
Corporal or Drummer	8d.
Common soldiers	6d.

During the first half of July the army advanced from Nottingham via Alcester to Pershore. The aim was 'to make a line from Chester to Shrewsbury, and from Shrewsbury to Hereford as good as that Auntient Trench called Offa's Dyke'. By 13 July they had arrived at Droitwich and crossed the Severn at Bewdley. By the 20th they were on the county border at Tenbury, and Leven went to Gloucester to make arrangements for heavier ordnance.

The Royalist base at Canon Frome stood in their way and had to be subjugated before any attempt could be made on Hereford. It was held by a resolute officer, one Colonel Barnold, who, on being invited to surrender, told Leven that he would defend the moated site as long as he had a drop of blood in his body—and proceeded to do so. There were only about 120 in the garrison and the Scots army made short work of the attack. About half of the defenders were killed during the action and 30 who attempted to flee were put to the sword. The rest were only saved by the approach of Lord Calendar, who had a reputation as a merciful commander.

The march continued, with the Earl of Leven complaining to Parliament about the state of the roads in Herefordshire, which he described as being the worst that the Scots had encountered, such that his army could only accomplish 8 miles in a day between Bromyard and Ledbury. By 23 July the headquarters of the Scots army was at Ledbury. From there, the army advanced towards Hereford in two brigades, 12 miles apart, arriving in front of the city on the 31st. They had some nine siege-pieces including three great brass guns that Leven had obtained from Gloucester.

The efforts that Scudamore had put in to improving the defences of Hereford were now to pay dividends. The city had ample provisions; the fortifications had been strengthened; gates had been stopped up and draw-bridges put in place and made to work; ammunition had been obtained and, most of all, the areas around the gates had been cleared of all possible obstacles. Hereford was as well prepared for a siege as could be.

It has been estimated that within the city, which then had a population of some 4,500, there were by then a total of some 1,500 soldiers and townsmen who were prepared to carry arms. This included many gentlemen who had retired on Hereford as areas under Royalist control became less and less. The city also possessed eleven pieces of ordnance with sufficient quantities of powder, ball and match.

The main information about the siege of Hereford is in the following letter which was written by Barnabas Scudamore to Lord Digby. It was eventually published as a pamphlet, being printed by Leonard Lichfield, printer to Oxford University, in 1645:

My Lord,

A Numerous and Active Army closely besieging us, hath rendered me, and those engaged with me, (in regard of perpetuall duty, without reliefe of Guards for five weeks together) incapable of presenting your Lordship with any exact Relation thereof; I can, therefore, hint it only for a better Mercury[1]. The Officers, Gentry (whereof I shall send a List), Clergy, Citizens, and Common Souldiers, behaved themselves all gallantly upon their duty, many eminently; to particularize each would be too great a trespasse on your Lordships more weighty affaires. Breifly, beleeve me, my Lord, the walls of their valiant breasts were all strongly lined with Courage and Loyalty.

On the 30th of July, I sent out a party of twenty Horse over Wye-bridge, who discovering their forlorne hope of horse, charged them into their maine Body, and retreated in very little disorder, and with losse only of one Trooper, (taken prisoner) some of the Scots falling. Immediatly after this, their whole Body of Horse faced us, about ten of the Clock in the morning, within the reach of our Cannon, and were welcomed with our mettall; good execution being done upon them, their Foot as yet undiscovered. About halfe an houre after, I caused a strong Party of Foot (seconded with Horse) to line the hedges, who galled them in their passage to the Fords, after whose handsome retreat, I began to ensafe the Ports, which I did that night. In the morning, appeared their Body of Foot, and we found our selves surrounded. I injoined the Bells silence, least their ringing, which was an Alarme to awaken our devotion,

---

1 A better and faster report, after Mercury, the messenger of the gods.

might Chime them together to the execution of their malice. For the same reason, I stopt our Clocks; and hereby, though I prevented their telling tales to the advantage of the Enemy, I myselfe lost the punctuall observation of many particulars, which, therefore, I must more confusedly relate unto your Lordship.

Before they attempted any thing against the Towne, they invited us to a Surrendre, and this they did by a double Summons, one from Leven, directed to me; the other from the Committee of both Kingdomes (attending upon the affaires of the Army) sent to the Mayor and Corporation: but we complyed so well in our Resolutions, that our positive answer served for both Parties, which was returned by me to their Generall.

This not giving that satisfaction they desired, they began to approach upon the first of August, but very slowly and modestly, as yet intending more the security of their owne persons than the ruine of ours: but all their Art could not protect them from our small and great shot which fell upon them. Besides this, our men galled them handsomly at their severall Sallies, over Wye-bridge; once beat them up to their maine guard, and at another demolisht one side of St. Martin's Steeple; which would have much annoyed us at the Bridge and Pallace; this was performed with the hurt of only two men, but with losse of great store of the Enemies men.

When they saw how difficult the Service would prove, before they could compasse their designes by force, they made use of another Engine which was flattery. The Major and Aldermen are courted to yeeld the Towne by an Epistle, subscribed by six of the Country Gentlemen, very compassionate and suasory: but upon our refusall to stoup to this lure, they were much incensed that they had been so long disappointed, and, having all this while continued their line of communication, they raised their Batteries, commencing at Wye-bridge, from whence they received the greatest dammage, but, instead of revenging that losse upon us, they multiplied their owne, by the death of their much-lamented Major Generall Crafford, and some others that fell with him. This provoked them to play hot upon the Gate for two dayes together, and battered it so much, (being the weakest) that it was rendered uselesse, yet our men stopt it up with Wooll-sacks and Timber, and, for our greater assurance of

To the Governour of the City of Hereford
SIR,
Our appearance before you in this posture, is for no other end, but the settling in truth, of peace with England, without the least desire to shed the bloud of any Subject in it; our by-past actions may be a sufficient proof hereof; Therefore this is to Summond and require you to deliver up that city unto me, to be kept for the use of his Majestie and the parliament of England: whereunto, if you shall be so wise and happy to condescend, you may have conditions honourable and safe; but if, otherwise, worse councell shall so farre prevaile with you, as to contemne this offer, I am perswaded all the world, and you also, will acquit me of the manifold inconveniences which will undoubtedly ensue upon your refusall. Consider hardly of your owne condition, and of those now under your charge, whose bloud will be laid upon your accompt, and returne an Answer within three houres after the receipt of this, unto me.
So sent at the Leaguer before Hereford, this last day of July, about ten of the clock in the forenoone.
LEVEN.

The first letter from the Earl of Leven to Sir Barnabas Scudamore written on 31 July

For the Mayor, Aldermen, and Commons of the City of Hereford,

GENTLEMEN,
Wee, the Commissioners appointed by the parliament of England, to reside in the Scots army, forseeing the great Miseries and Calamities that are likely to ensue to this city of Hereford, in the case the Summons sent by his Excellency the Earle of Leven, shall be refused by the Governour, have thought good to give you timely advice to use your uttermost endeavours, that a positive and satisfactory Answer may be returned thereunto, lest that by a wilfull delay or refusall, you bring utter ruine and destruction, not only to your selves, but to all that are with you, which will not lie in the power of any to prevent.
                    Your Loving friends,
From the Leaguer before Hereford, July 31, 1645
JOHN CORBETT, WILLIAM PULFREY, EDWARD BAYNTON. HUMFREY SALWEY.

The accompanying letter from the Parliamentary Commissioners resident with the Scots army

My Lord,

I am not to give up the King's Garrison upon any Summons or Letter, neither shall it be in the power of the Mayor or other to condescend to any such Proposition made unto him. I was set in here by the King's Command, and shall not quit it but by speciall order from His Majesty or the Prince. And with this resolution I shall persist in Hereford

This last of July, 1645.   BARNABAS SCUDAMORE

Scudamore's reply to the previous two letters

SIR,

By a former addresse I made knowne unto you the constant desires and resolutions of this army to shun the effusion of bloud, and to preserve cities and families from desolation; and for that end did invite you to a peaceful surrender of that city, for the use of his Majestie and the Parliament of England, upon conditions honourable and safe, whereby they might enjoy the fruits of a settled peace, which other garrisons which have been in the like condition now doe; whereunto, upon grounds best known unto yourselfe, you thought it not then fitting to condescend. Nevertheless, that I may convince you of the realities of our desires and resolutions before mentioned, and of you owne guilti-nesse of all the bloudshed, misery, and desolation, which your obstinacy may draw upon the persons, families, and estates of those people who are now under your charge, I have hereby once more resolved to renew my former offer, expecting you answer against tomorrow morning by six of the clocke, assuring you that if the opportunity be not laid hold of, but rejected, the like will not be offered unto you by

Leaguer, Aug 28th,   Your friend,
Five a'clock in the Afternoone   LEVEN

Leven's attempt to persuade Scudamore to agree terms at the end of August

My Lord,

For your favourable proffer to the inhabitants of this city, I shall returne their thankes, and resolution that they intend to suffer with me, and I shall not suffer alone for the effusion of bloud. I am sorry to think of it, that two united nations should so much differ, having paid once well for Scotland's friendship. My Lord, I am resolved to endure all mines and stormes which shall be made against this place, and doubt not, by God's assistance, to render his Majestie a good account of it; the which by my endea-vours I shall maintaine to the last, and remaine

Your lordships servant,   B. SCUDAMORE

Scudamore's indignant reply

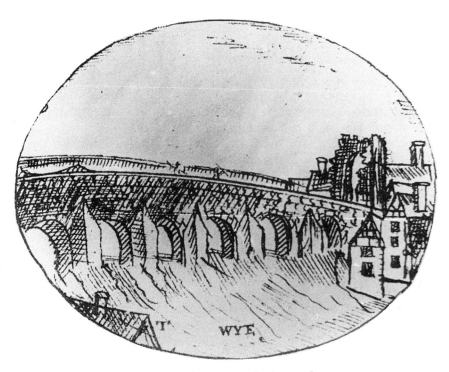

Wye Bridge in 1687, showing the damaged gateway

eluding their attempt, we brake an Arch, and raised a very strong Worke behind it.

The Enemy, frustrate of his hopes here, raiseth two severall Batteries, one at the Fryers, the other on the other side of Wye river, and from both these, plays his Ordinance against the corner of the wall by Wye side; but we repair and line our walls faster that they can batter them, whereupon they desist.

About the 11th of August, we discover a Mine at Frein-gate [probably Friars Gate], and imploy workmen to countermine them. When we had stopt the progresse of that Mine on one side of the Gate, they carried it on the other; which we also defeated by making a Sally-Port: and issuing forth did break it open and fire it.

About the 13th, they raise Batteries round about the Town, and make a Bridge over Wye River. The 14th, Doctor Scudamore is sent by them to desire admittance for three Country Gentlemen, who pretended in their Letters to import something of consequence to the good of the City and County. Free leave of ingresse and egresse was allowed them, but being admitted, their suggestions were found to us so frivolous and impertinent, that they were dismissed not without some disrelish and neglect; and the said Doctor, after they were past the Port, comming back from his company, was unfortunately slaine by a shot from the Enemy.[2]

About the 16th, they discover the face of their Battery against Frein-gate, with five severall gun-ports; from hence they played foure Cannon joyntly at our walls, and made a breach, which was instantly made up; they doe the like on the other side with the like successe.

The 17th, a notable Sally was made at St. Owen's Church with great execution, and divers Prisoners taken, with the losse only of one man; at which time little boyes strived which should first carry Torches and Faggots to fire their works, which was performed to some purpose, and so it was at the same Sally-port once before, though with a fewer number, and therefore with lesse execution.

And I may not forget to acquaint your Lordship with those other foure Sallies, made by us at the Castle to good effect: and what emulation there was between the Souldiers and Citizens, which should be most ingaged in them. Now their losse of Prisoners, slaughter of men, and dishonour of being beaten out of their workes, which they found ready to flame about their eares, if they returned presently into them, had so kindled their indignation, that presently they raysed Batteries against St. Owen's Church, and plaid fiercely at it, but to little purpose, which they so easily perceived, that from the 20th unto the 27th there was a great calme on all sides; we as willing to provide ourselves and preserve our ammunition for a storme, as they could be industrious or malitious to bring it upon us. Yet I cannot say either side was idle; for they ply'd their Mine at Saint Owen's, and prepared for Scaling; we countermined, imploy'd our boyes by day and night to steale out and fire their Workes, securing their retreat under the protection of our Musquetiers upon the wall, and what our fire could not perfect, (though it burnt farr and suffocated some of their Miners) our water did, breaking in upon them and drowning that which the fire had

---

2 It was later in the evening, following his return to the camp, that Dr. Rowland Scudamore was killed. Aparently he was waiting between the town and the trenches for a Mrs. Skinner who wished to talk with him. He was shot dead, but whether the bullet came from the city defenders or the Scotch trenches is unknown.

not consumed; and this saved us the pains of pursuing a mine, which we had sunk on purpose to render theirs in that place ineffectuall.

The 29th, Leven (a Mercifull Generall) assayes the Towne againe by his last offer of honourable conditions to surrender, but he found us still unrelenting, the terror of his Cannon making no impression at all upon our Spirits, though the bullets discharged from them had done so much against our walls: this (though some of their chiefe Commanders were remisse and coole at the debate and some contradictory) drives their greatest spirits into a passionate resolution of storming.

And to that purpose August 30th, and September 1st they prepare ladders, hurdles, and other accommodations for the advancing their designe, and securing their persons in the attempt, and played very hot with their Cannon upon Bysters-gate, and the halfe moon next St. Owen's-gate, intending the morrow after to fall on; presuming, as they boasted, that, after they had rung us this passing peale, they should presently force the Garrison to give up her Loyall Ghost. But the same night his Majesty advancing from Worcester, gave them a very hot alarum, and drawing a little neerer to us, like the Sunne to the Meridian, this Scottish mist beganne to disperse, and the next morning vanished out of sight.

My Lord, I should give your Lordship an account of the valor of our common Souldiers and Townesmen, that would hazard themselves at the making up of breaches (to the astonishment of the Enemy) till their Cannon played between their leggs; and even the Women (such was their gallantry) ventred where the Musquet bullets did soe. And I should acquaint your Honour, what frequent alarums we gave them by fire-balls, lights upon our Steeple, by Dogs, Cats, and outworne Horses, having light Matches tyed about them and turned out upon their works; whereby we put the enemy in such distraction, that sometimes they charged one another: this recreation we had in the middest of our besieging: and one morning, instead of beating Reveillie, we had a crye of Hounds, in pursuit after the traine of a Fox about the Walls of the Citty, so little were we dismaied at the threats or attempts of them. I may not forget one remarkable peece of Divine Providence, that God sent us singular men of all professions, very usefull, and necessary to us in this distresse, and so accidentally to us, as if they had on purpose been let downe from heaven to serve our present and emergent occasions: such as skilfull Miners, excellent Cannoneers (one whereof spent but one shot in vaine throughout the whole Siedge) an expert Carpenter [probably John Abel], the only man in all the Country to make Mills, without whom we had been much disfurnisht of a meanes to make Powder (after our Powder-mill was burnt) or grind Corne, That providence that brought these to us, at last drove our Enemies from us, after the destruction of four or five Mines, (which since appeares to be their number) the expence of three hundred Cannon shot, besides other Ammunition spent with Muskets, the losse (by their owne confession) of twelve hundred, and as the Country sayes two thousand, men: we, in all, not loosing above twenty-one by all Casualties whatsoever.

Thus craving your Lordships pardon for my prolixity, I take leave and rest

Your Lordship's most humble servant,

BAR. SCUDAMORE

To the Right Hon. the Lord Digby.

During the siege of Hereford the Scots army, according to Leven, lost 1,200 men. Others suggest that the true figure was nearer 2,000. Within the city, Scudamore lost not more than 21.

One problem that has never been satisfactorily resolved is the extent of the lines built by the Scots army during their six week siege of Hereford. There is little primary documentary evidence although later sources provide some information. The problem is a common one throughout the country for, once the war was over, Parliament issued orders to ensure that any works built during the war could not be used again by any opposing troops. As a result of these instructions ditches were infilled and ramparts levelled. Any traces which were left must have been only slight reminders of the original massive works. On top of this there has been 350 years of erosion, damage by plough and other levelling operations to be considered. The published works of the late 19th century antiquarians such as Price and Duncumb, writing only 150 years after the events, are of considerable value.

Price describes how the Scots 'having erected numerous batteries, began to cannonade in a terrible manner, their guns on the south side of the river Wye, played upon the Castle, Cathedral, Palace and Chapter-

Week one

Mon 28 July	Commissioners of Scottish Army meet at Gloucester and agree to the attack on Hereford.
Tues 29 July	Scottish army moves towards Hereford.
Wed 30 July	Army headquarters at Fownhope; Horse reach the city 10am. Scudamore welcomes them with cannon fire.
Thur 31 July	Scottish foot appear at Hereford and the city is surrounded; Leven demands the surrender of the city and is refused.
Fri 1 Aug	Scots dig in and prepare their huts; Leven sends for battering pieces from Gloucester. Scudamore continues to fire on them. Sallies over Wye Bridge; part of St Martins steeple destroyed.
Sat 2 Aug	Part of Samuel Aubrey's house called the Abbey, which was west of the city and on banks of the Wye is taken by the Scots. (This was presumably the manor house of the Aubreys at Clehonger that was replaced by the present Belmont in 1788 following a fire.) The embankment in Below Eign suburb is constructed and the earthwork across Bishop's Meadow strengthened.

Week two

Mon 4 Aug	Cannonades from the castle at intervals. Wye Bridge Gate is damaged to the extent that it is useless for defence so the townsfolk break out an arch of the bridge and build a strong work behind it. Major General Crafford of the Scottish army is killed.
Tue 5 Aug	Scots batteries being prepared. Commissioners view the works.
Wed 6 Aug	Nine pieces of ordnance arrive from Gloucester.
Thur 7 Aug	One of the Gloucester pieces is used against the city but with little effect.
Fri 8 Aug	Lieut-Col Gordon (an engineering officer with the Scots) is killed whilst viewing the city with his prospecting glass.
Sat 9 Aug	Sir David Leslie and 4,000 horse depart under orders from Parliament on the way to Newark.

THE SIEGE

Week three

Mon 11Aug	A mine is discovered at Friars Gate and a countermine is dug. A second mine in the same area is defeated by a foray through a sally-port and firing it.
Tues 12 Aug	Powder arrives from Gloucester & Northampton.
Wed 13 Aug	Preparations are made for a full assault on the city including building a new bridge built across the Wye.
Thur 14 Aug	Leven announces his forthcoming assault and some negotiations follow. Later in the day Dr. Rowland Scudamore (a Scots negotiator) is accidentally killed.
Fri 15 Aug	The 'great assault' begins with an attack on Friars Gate using four cannon against the walls.
Sat 16 Aug	Renewed assault again with a total lack of success.
Sun 17 Aug	A quiet day apart from a midnight sally to St Owen's Church when the attackers works are fired.

Weeks four & five

Mon 18 Aug	The Scots raise new batteries and St Owen's Church is ruined.
Tues 19 Aug	The Scots continue to destroy St Owen's Church.
Wed 20-Tues 26 Aug	A week of continual rain that dampened the ardour of both sides. Leven is awaiting ammunition. The townsmen are high-spirited and even have a fox-hunt on the walls. During one sally 100 Scots are slain.
Wed 27 Aug	Bullets & Powder arrive for the Earl of Leven.
Thur 28 Aug	The Scots make a two cart wide breach in the wall but it is made up again before an assault could be mounted.
Fri 29 Aug	The Earl sends another demand to surrender which is spurned.
Sat 30 Aug	Scots hold a council of war—after much discussion they agree an attempt to storm the town again.
Sun 31 Aug	Preparations made for the next assault.

Week six

Mon 1 Sept	The Scots attempt Bye Street Gate with their cannon and St. Owen's Gate with their battery, but with news of the king's potential arrival they withdraw their army to the open fields.
Tues 2 Sept	The Scots retreat to Fownhope.
Wed 3 Sept	The Scots army arrives at Newent.
Thur 4 Sept	The king arrives in Hereford.

The City Of Hereford

All Saints · Hereford Cathedral · Widemarsh Gate · Blackfriars · St Peters · Bye Street Gate

St Guthlac's Priory · St Owen's Gate · St Owens

GENERAL EARL OF LEVEN

Bartonsham

Wye Brigg · Friar's Gate · Eignbate · St Nicholas · Greyfriars · St Martins · The Gate · River Wye · Bishop's Meadow · Hereford Castle

THE DESCRIPTION OF THE SCOT'S ARMIE AT THE SIEGE OF HEREFORD
Earl of Leven's Horse & Foot, as they were drawn, with several leaders to worke the day TENTH day Aug 1645

PER BYRON

0 · 100 · 150 · 200 · 250
A SCALE OF PACES

A modern representation of the siege of Hereford. The Scots' leaguer is in the Bartonsham area
between the long bend in the River Wye and the Row Ditch embankment

102

house, the latter of which, a noble and elegant structure, was almost entirely destroyed.' He appreciated that they 'had pitched their tents about a quarter of a mile south-east of the city, in some common fields, now called Bassom or Bartonsham Meadows, where several remains of their entrenchments are yet visible. Pieces of swords, gun-locks, &c. are oftentimes picked up there, by those who till the ground.'

Duncumb, who began to publish his monumental *Collections towards the History and Antiquities of the County of Hereford* a few years later goes into more detail, describing how 'amongst other operations deemed necessary by the besiegers, during their attempt on the city, a strong parapet, or breast-work of earth, was thrown up across a neck of land, from a point of the river Wye, in the Below-Eigne suburb, to another point of the river, about three hundred yards below the castle, being an extent of eight hundred yards, nearly in a right line from east to west.' This is the earthwork, called Row Ditch, of which traces still remain just beyond the ends of the gardens of the houses on the south side of Park Street. The ditch that must have been a prominent feature on the north side of the embankment has totally disappeared, but Duncumb could estimate that 'the parapet, in its original state, measured twenty feet in height from the bottom of the fosse.'

The earthwork crossed the narrow part of a large bend in the river Wye and with this work in front and with the river encircling the rear, the intermediate position must have been one of considerable security. Duncumb also appreciated that 'works of similar construction, but of less extent, were carried out in a meadow still nearer the city, and opposite the east wall of the castle; but these and others, in different places, have since been wholly obliterated.' Houses and gardens now cover these buried earthworks to the east of the castle and their positions can only be conjectured.

On the opposite side of the river to the castle, the Row Ditch line is continued through Bishop's Meadow. This earthwork, which originally crossed St. Martin's Street and then turned north towards the river, was built, probably in the 13th century, as a defence for the St. Martin's suburb on the south side of the Wye. This suburb was abandoned to the besiegers during the Civil War, and the Row Ditch earthwork was used by them as a protection against the cannon from the castle. It may well have been the Scots army that infilled the ditch that ran on the south side to make it easier to use in attacks on the city. Duncumb mentions that 'human skeletons have frequently been met with in levelling these parapets.'

Because of the regular sallies by the defenders, a considerable proportion of the besieging force was stationed by the Scottish commander on the eminences of Dinedor and Aconbury, the former at the distance of

Wye Bridge, showing the arch rebuilt after the siege on the right

two, and the latter at the distance of four, miles from the city. Duncumb considered that 'fresh works were thrown up on the lines of the old intrenchments there, and from thence the country was laid under heavy contributions for the support of their army.' Names such as Scotch-bridge and Scotch-bridge-furlongs are still met with in Dinedor; and human bones, (probably the remains of those who died at this period) have occasionally been discovered in the camp at Aconbury.

John Webb, writing half a century later, merely quotes the works of Price and Duncumb without adding to the story, but Richard Johnson, in a footnote to his *Ancient Customs of the City of Hereford* mentions that: 'at the beginning of the present century [the 19th] there was to be seen in a meadow near Eigne, eastward of this city, a wide entrance leading to a subterranean passage called Scots' Hole, and within the memory of persons yet living it has been explored for some distance in the direction of Hereford. Near this place bullets have been dug up. Some antiquaries have supposed the passage to be a mine made by the Scots during this siege; others, that it was an underground communication from St. Guthlac's priory to the Vineyard, where it is said a religious establishment was formerly situated.'

Scots' Hole still survives as a deep depression in the ground, rather like a quarry but with relatively smooth grass-covered sides, in the eastern part of the city adjacent to Old Eign Hill. In addition to its use by the Scots, it is suggested that Colonel Birch's troops hid there a little later in the Civil War.

Rev. Webb includes in his *Memorials of the Civil War in Herefordshire* an appendix of traditions of the Civil War. These traditions were collected by the elder Webb and edited by his son. To consider their relevance, it has to be appreciated that the Rev. John Webb was born in the 18th century and lived to the age of some 93 years. He first reported on his researches at a meeting of the Society of Antiquaries in 1836—the result of 'many years of thoughtful study'. A note indicates that this section had been put together by 1825. Although it is now 350 years since the siege of Hereford, when Webb was discussing the events with older people at the time, they were relating stories that they had heard many years previously, but first-hand, from their grandparents. The first section of the appendix deals with traditions that Webb considers to be 'simply absurd'. Even so, they make delightful reading and some are included for that reason alone.

He quotes a story he heard that a 'mortar-piece having been fixed at St. Nicholas' Church [then in the middle of the road at the junction of Bridge Street and King Street] and loaded to the mouth with rusty nails, old iron, bits of glass, &c., the gate at Wye-bridge was opened, and the enemy invited to enter.' There was also the story that the Scots attempted to undermine the river, but 'the water was let in upon them, and their bodies remain in the mine to this day.'

More probable is the story that Webb heard many times that 'the mining was first discovered by an old woman who heard the sound under foot as she sat at her spinning-wheel, or that a drummer, or an old blind soldier, ascertained the exact spot by putting down a drum, with peas, or a boy's marble, upon it, which danced at the miner's stroke; so that they opened the town-ditch into the mine and drowned it.' There is also the story of the bull that was 'covered with hurds and pitch, fired by the tail, and sent loose out of one of the gates.' This tends to be in accordance with Scudamore's statements about a similar use of dogs, cats and horses, though considerably more alarming.

Webb also talked to a William Town whom he described as a quaint old farmer from Tretire-with-Michaelchurch and as an unusually reliable authority. Town said that 'his father knew a baker named Rodd in Hereford, who asserted that it was his master who shot the Scottish General through a lancet-hole, as he was riding round the walls upon a grey horse.' The same informant also said that 'during the siege the Scots ordered all the neighbouring parishes to each send a cart-load of provisions every week: the parish of Wellington, where his ancestors lived, used to send one. If a man and a boy attended the cart, they regularly kept the man and sent the boy back with the cart. At last the parish sent an old woman with the weekly load. One day as she was going by Morton (or Marden), the water of the Warey brook being much out, the cart was upset in the deep water and carried down the stream, and the old woman and two horses were drowned: she was found next morning entangled in the wheels.'

Webb saw a long duck-gun at The Moor, the family seat of the Penoyres in the parish of Clifford. Aged persons at the end of the last century used to say that it was used to shoot a Scot 'from the walls, as he was sitting outside, or on, the trenches and combing his hair.'

Records of individual events are often embellished as time goes on, but the traditions connected with the plunderings of the Scots seem to be of a much more consistent and reliable character. To supply an army with the necessary food and provisions has always been one of the major difficulties of warfare. The Scots army included Commissioners, appointed by Parliament, whose responsibility was to requisition the necessary supplies. In this they were unsuccessful and as a result the Scots were compelled to take the remedy in their own hands. The Civil War had resulted in suffering throughout the country but Webb asserted that no other county was 'more systematically plundered than that of Hereford.' Whilst the foot soldiers bore the brunt and burden of the siege, the horse quartered the whole area to obtain food and provisions. Parish after parish was visited and the outcry was universal. The whole population of the county were infuriated against the Parliament and their 'dear brethren' of the North.

The problem was one that is common to all raiding parties; the Scots did not confine themselves to the bare necessities of life and the exigencies of war, taking just grain, oxen, sheep and horses; in addition they went through the buildings taking whatever caught their fancy. They plundered, but did not kill wantonly; an account collected from most of the parishes in the county by Miles Hill[3], and published some five years later, does not mention loss of life or cruelty, though it does charge the raiders with rapacity.

Webb gives several examples of stories which were passed down by parents to their children through the generations. He records that at Treago Castle, the ancient seat of the Mynors family 'as the Scots were

3 Miles Hill, a Herefordshire solicitor who had been entrusted by the parliamentary commissioners with the management of their provisions, explicitly states that though 'an orderly course was taken for their subsistance, far above the ability of that poore County' they pleaded dissatisfaction as a pretext for plundering the county at their pleasure. His report appears in the next chapter.

St. Owen's Gate as sketched in 1784

descending the hill, they were observed by the inmates, and preparation
was made for their reception. The owner, who was a Royalist, seems to
have been absent, but his wife, the grandmother of Mrs. Parry of Arkstone,
who related the story to the person from whom I heard it in 1827, with
judicious presence of mind caused the doors to be thrown open, and
welcomed them as friends.' Apparently the Scots officers were 'delighted
with their entertainment and with the manners of the lady who presided.
She even assumed an air of cheerfulness, and condescended to amuse
them by singing and accompanying her voice with a musical instrument.'

The ruse must have been successful for the soldiers departed and for courtesy and the lady's sake Treago was spared from pillage. The story may well be true—there is no account of Treago or of the adjoining parish of St. Weonard's in the list of plundered places.

Another story came from Mary Howels, who was aged 86 in 1834. She had heard from her mother what occurred at Llansilo forge, where her grandmother's sister lived as a girl. Apparently her father, Richard Kemble, was clerk of the ironworks there as well as those at the furnace at St. Weonard's, which were occupied by the same person. The story goes that 'one day the cloke-bag containing the money to pay the workmen had just been brought there, and was lying on the table, when a body of plunderers were seen to approach the house: the girl immediately wrapped it up in a dirty cloth, carried it out through the soldiers, and threw it unobserved into the hog-tub.'

Another story that has the ring of truth about it was told by John Hughes, aged 85. His grandmother was 15 years of age and living near Wormelow Tump when the Scots army had their camp on Aconbury Hill, the commander's tent being on the very summit. She said that they 'brought the cattle that they drove off to Wormelow Tump and slaughtered them there.' She also recollected that the people of the house made a hole under a pear tree to bury their bacon and pewter, and it was not discovered. (Several hoards of coins of Civil War date have been found in the south of the county, having been deliberately buried.)

The defence of Hereford was a serious business during the siege and all the citizens were expected to support the cause. Sallies were a regular event and after one of them a Mrs. Hyde was arrested for giving away its time and place. Apparently she was a widow with a small son and did it for money. This was not considered an adequate excuse and a little later she was hanged. Surprisingly, she was buried in the cathedral burial ground, and her tombstone could still be seen up to the turn of the century.

Another interment was recorded on a flat stone in the south-east aisle of the cathedral by Duncumb. The inscription read:

Here lieth the body of Philip Trahearne, whose fidelity and constancy to the injured cause of King Charles I, fervent zeal for the established church and clergy, friendly and affectionate behaviour and conversation, rendered him highly valuable to all the loyal party. He was twice Mayor of this city, and a principal agent in its defence against the Scots. He died October 17, 1645, aged 79.

CHAPTER EIGHT

After the Siege

At the beginning of August, the king was at Cardiff and had some 2,000 cavalry between Monmouth and Raglan and a further 3,000 towards Ludlow. It was here that he received the alarming news from Hereford that the Scots army had encircled the city. This news was bad enough, but more was to follow. On 5 August, Haverfordwest, in the south-west of Wales, was taken by storm by a small parliamentary army. The king appreciated that his condition was becoming precarious and, with the troops to hand, could do nothing whatsoever to help Hereford.

He decided to attempt to join with Montrose in the north, but first he had to pass the Scots besieging Hereford. With his small army, he made his way over the hills, first to Brecon and then for a night at Old Radnor, 'where ye King lay in a poor low Chamber, & my Lord of Linsey and others by ye Kitchen fire on hay.' From there he made his way to the relative civilisation of Ludlow and thence north to Doncaster. He did not meet up with Montrose, but, hearing that David Leslie was near, he returned down the eastern side of the country through Newark to Stamford and Huntingdon and then across country to arrive in Oxford on 28 August.

He was still anxious to relieve Hereford and only spent two nights in Oxford before making his way westwards again. On 30 August he was at Moreton-in-Marsh and the following day, with a great effort, he reached Worcester. He stayed there two days and was reinforced by some of Prince Maurice's horse. From there it was but a short journey to Bromyard where he spent the night of 3 September.

By this time the forces around Hereford had received intelligence of the king's imminent arrival and, according to Hereford's Governor, Barnabas

Scudamore, 'this Scottish mist beganne to disperse, and the next morning vanished out of sight.'

Lord Clarendon noted that the king had 'received information that the Scotch army, upon notice of his purpose, was that morning risen in great disorder and confusion, and resolved to make their retreat on the Welsh side of the river, and so to pass to Gloucester. This news was so welcome, and his majesty was received with so much joy into the city of Hereford, that he slipped the opportunity he then had of discommoding, if not ruining, the Scotch army.' Clarendon was suggesting that the king should have attempted the destruction of the Scots army, but he may have been wise not to make the attempt, for he had only a force of cavalry, whilst the Scots, although mauled during the siege, had an effective and superior force of infantry. The king approached Hereford on the Bromyard road on 4 September whilst the Scots, who had abandoned the Hereford siege two days earlier, retreated on the right bank of the Wye towards Ross. This would have secured them from a flank attack from the English side of the river as there was no bridge before Ross. They would then have had to cross the river by Wilton Bridge, built in 1600, in order to reach Ross. The bridge had been broken down at the king's order, but had been repaired by the Scots in order to preserve their line of retreat. By 5 September they were in Gloucester.

It is worth examining the diary of the king's movements for the period after the siege, as he endeavoured to come to the relief of his other forces and, at the same time, stay out of the hands of the various parliamentary armies that were scouring the area for him:

Wed. 3 Sept.	Moved from Worcester to Bromyard, staying the night at Mrs. Baynham's; the army lay in the field.
Thurs. 4 Sept.	Went with his own regiment to Hereford where he had dinner and spent the night in the bishop's palace. His advance guard spent the night at Madley.
Fri. 5 Sept.	Went to Leominster and had dinner at the Unicorn. He then went on to Weobley where he had supper at the Unicorn there and spent the night.
Sat. 6 Sept.	Returned to Hereford and again had dinner at the bishop's palace. His advance guard spent the night at Letton.
Sun. 7 Sept.	Moved to Raglan Castle, hoping to organise the relief of Bristol. By this time his advance guards were at Tredegar. He spent the week there, visiting Abergavenny twice. On his second visit on Thursday 11 Sept., his business was to

'comitt five chief hinderers of that county from releaving Hereford.' At Raglan he had the bad news that Bristol had fallen to the parliamentarian troops and on the 12th he went some way towards Hereford, but then returned to Raglan.

Sun. 14 Sept.   He left Raglan, never to return, and made his way to Monmouth where he had dinner with the governor and then went on to Hereford in the evening. From Hereford he sent orders for all the officers and their troops in the counties of Salop, Worcester, and South Wales, to attend him at Hereford. He also wrote an angry letter to Prince Rupert, who had commanded Bristol and had assured the king that he could defend it for four months, but surrendered in as many days. The prince was relieved of his command and eventually left the country. Charles's next problem was in the north where Chester was in need of deliverance.

Mon. 15 Sept.   As a first attempt at the relief of Chester, he marched half-way to Bromyard, probably hoping to meet up with Gerrard's horse in Ludlow. He was unsuccessful, possibly because of parliamentary cavalry led by Poyntz in the Leominster area. He returned to Hereford for the night.

Tues. 16 Sept.   Spent the day in Hereford, sending messengers for Langdale to bring his horse out of Wales to quarters at Byford.

Wed. 17 Sept.   Arranged a rendezvous at Arthur's Stone above Dorstone. By this time Poyntz was at Weobley, and this meeting in a remote part of western Herefordshire may have been a feint or a genuine intention to advance on Chester by crossing the Radnorshire hills. Whatever the objective, the king dined there and then returned to Holme Lacy where he had supper and spent the night.

Thurs. 18 Sept. Chester was well out of reach so Charles decided to aim for Worcester. He advanced as far as Stoke Edith, but found that Poyntz had marched throughout the night to inter-cept him. Once again, he headed for the hills and turned north-westwards, crossing the River Arrow between Marden and Wellington, passing through Leominster and Weobley without daring to stop, and finally ending up for the night in Presteigne. The march had lasted from six in the morning until midnight. Here the king left Herefordshire, travelling via Newtown and Chirk Castle on his way to his unsuccessful attempt to relieve Chester.

Charles in Hereford

When Charles entered the city on 4 September it was reported that 'Hereford and the whole county were transported with exaltation and triumph.' The church bells, that had been silenced during the long siege, were made to peal out again. Indeed, at All Saints Church, the church wardens' accounts show a payment for 'Ringing for the King'—presumably part of the celebration for his triumphal arrival.

Immediately afterwards, there was the usual 'witch hunt' to root out those who had supported the parliamentary cause. The king issued a warrant to the Governor to imprison the favourers of the Scots throughout the county. He was also allowed to indemnify himself and his officers for the expenses they had suffered during the siege, from the property and goods of the parliamentary supporters. Such supporters had to fly the county and 'wives and children turned out of all, some of their houses burnt. They were so mad that Mr. Guilliam of Wellington had but little corn or hay in his barn, but they cryed he had given it all away to the Scots, and so set fire on it and burnt it down.'

The king had little that he could offer personally, but he obviously appreciated the tremendous efforts that Barnabas Scudamore had put into the defence of the city and on Thursday 4 September, his first day in Hereford, he acknowledged his debt by granting him a knighthood. Jane Merricke was also presented to the king. She had been in charge of one of the gangs of women helping to repair the defences in the St. Owen's Gate area when she had been badly injured by splinters when a cannon ball hit the wall near by. Many years later when she attempted to gain recompense for her injuries, she remembered that the king had said that all would be rewarded for their sacrifices in his cause.

But it was to the city as a whole that Charles wanted to show his gratitude. This was done by an augmentation to the city's coat of arms. It was granted by the king on 16 September, 1645, whilst he was in the throes of organising his few troops to go to the relief of Chester.

The three lions are those of Richard I, and the new border with ten saltires on a blue background was to commemorate the ten Scottish regiments that took part in the siege. The motto 'Invictæ Fidelitatis Præmium' translates as 'The reward for faithfulness unconquered.' The lion crest on top of the coat of arms (defender of the faith) is very rare in civic heraldry. Of even greater rarity is the gold-barred peer's helm; this is found only in one other municipal authority—the City of London.

During the siege, it was not just the city that suffered; the Scots army did an immense amount of damage for many miles around during the six weeks that they invested Hereford. A committee had been appointed by

INVICTÆ FIDELITATIS PRÆMIUM

Parliament to supply them with provisions, but, bearing in mind the numbers involved, failure could have been predicted. The army was left largely to its own resources and had to seek subsistence wherever possible and it was only after the conflict was finally over that the full extent of its depredations could be properly appreciated. It is well shown in the following pamphlet, published in 1650:

> A true and impartiall accounte of the plunderings, losses, and sufferings of the county of Hereford by the Scottish army, during their siege before the city of Hereford, Anno Dom. 1645, since brought in by the country in writing; published in this juncture of time for the undeceiving of the people, who may perhaps fancy to themselves some unimaginable advantages by

The Patent of the addition to the Coat-Armour of the ancient and truly loyall City of Hereford

To all and singular unto whom these presents shall come Sir Edward Walker, knight, Garter Principal King of Arms of Englishmen, sendeth greeting.

Whereas it is not agreeable to justice and reason that those persons, families, or cities that have excelled in wisdome, fidelitie, and eminent service to their prince and countrey in times of warr should have no due regard for such their worthy and valiant actions; and as the barbarous multitude of rebells and their many and traitorous practices against his Majesties sacred person, the religion, laws, and liberties of his Majesties kingdomes, hath excelled the example of former ages, and have thereby rendered the duty, courage, and loyaltie of those who have valiantlie and faithfully adhered to his Majestie the more perspicuous and deserving esteem, so there hath not any city since the beginning of this unnaturall rebellion expressed greater fidelitie and courage than the city of Hereford in continuing their allegiance and resisting the many attempts of the rebells. But the greatness of their loyaltie, courage, and undaunted resolution did then most eminently appear when, being strictly beseiged for the space of five weeks by a powerfull army of rebellious Scots and having no hopes of relief, they joineing with the garrison and doing the duty of souldiers then defended themselves and repell'd their fury and assaults with such singular constance and resolution, and with such great destruction of the beseigers as that they are thereby become the wonder of their neighbouring garrisons and may be an example to all other cities, and therefore do justly deserve such characters of honour as may certifie to posteritie.

Know ye, therefore, that I the sayd Sir Edward Walker, knight, Garter Principal King at Arms of Englishmen, by the power and authority annexed to my office of Garter, and confirmed to me by his Majesties letters patent under the great seal of England, and likewise his especiall command and direction, have devised and sett forth such an addition and augmentation of arms, with crest, supporters, and motto, unto and for the said citty, and by whom it was beseiged, viz:—

About the ancient arms of the citty, being Gules, three lions passant gardant argent: on a bordure azure x. cross saltiers or Scottish crosses argent; supported by two lions rampant gardant argent, each collered azure, and on each collar three buckles or, in reference to the armes of the rebellious general Lesley, Earle of Leven; and for the crest, on a helme and torse of the cullars, mantled gules, doubled argent, a lion passant gardant argent holding in his right paw a sword erected proper, hilted and pomelled or; and in an escroule underneath this motto, 'Invictœ fidelitatis prœmium.'

Which augmentation of arms, crest, supporters, and motto, I do hereby grant and assign unto the now mayor, aldermen, and corporation of the citty of Hereford, to be by them and their successors for ever set forth upon all occasions as the proper arms of the citty.

In witness thereof I have hereunto subscribed my name and affixed the seale of my office this sixteenth day of September, in the one and twentieth year of the reign of our sovereign Charles, by the grace of God king of England, Scotland, France, and Ireland, defender of the faith &c., and in the year of our Lord 1645.

stickling for the Scots and their partizans in this nation. By Miles Hill, gent. London, 1650.

To the Christian reader: an abstract taken of the losses, dammages, and plunderings of one hundred and six small parishes within the county of Hereford, by the Scottish army commanded by General Leven, in which the poor inhabitants thereof lost, as by a true accompt ready to be attested upon oath, under the hands of the officers and chief of every parish, appeareth, in which county are seventy parishes more which suffered in the like nature, as much, if not more, as is verily believed, which brought not in their accompts to be put to public view by reason of some disaffected to the business, being Scotified persons, in the prosecution of which were divers houses rifled, doors, chests, and trunks broken open, severall families undone, most of all their cattle, horses, and goods taken from them, much money, plate, jewels, and all things of rich household stuffe, rings, and other rich commodities, as wearing apparrel, linnen, books, the plate and linnen of divers churches, neere all the horses, mares and colts that ever they set their eyes upon, as wel from friends as others, which the reader may see if he please in an inventory as it was taken and brought in writing unto Miles Hill, gentleman, at the city of Hereford, in the moneth of September 1646, being the severall accompts of each parish, at the Major man's house at the signe of the boote, hard by the Fountaine taverne in the Strand; these outrages being committed in July and August the year before, as they lay in siege before the city of that county. Their body of foote had then close begirt it, who had their provisions brought in to them by the poor countrymen, they consisting of nine thousand and odd persons; their horse that guarded these foote were about fifteen hundred, David Lesley having marched with the rest towards Scotland. As soon as they entered the county, the spoyle being divided, most of it by those horses left to guard, these foote, there being many hundred of women and baggage-horses ready to receive it, who packed it up, who did constantly march with this army. Reader, if thou hadst been present to see the cryes these poor people made, if thy heart had not been hard, it would have melted into tears with them; considering that this army, coming in with the prayers of the kirke as brethren, should doe such things, and all within the space of thirty-six days. The siege began the 29th of July, 1645, and rose up the 2nd of September following, and left the city unattempted or taken.

The inventory is very full; just a few examples in the neighbourhood of Hereford will suffice to show the extent of the losses that were suffered by relatively small parishes during this six week period:

Taken and plundered from the parishioners of Mordeford
    to the value of   £490 0s. 0d.
Taken and plundered from the inhabitants of Holmer
    to the value of   £531 7s. 4d.
Taken and plundered from the inhabitants of Hampton Bishop
    to the value of   £511 18s. 4d.
Taken and plundered from the inhabitants of Dineder
    to the value of   £484   7s. 8d.

The author goes on to calculate the loss throughout the county. He estimates that 'besides the dammage, plundering, and losses of the seventy parishes which brought not in their accounts, with divers gentlemen and persons that neglected to bring in their accounts that lived within the one hundred and six parishes herein accounted for, which is expected might have amounted neere the summe of £30,000 more: the totall of the whole is £61,743 5s. 2d.'

Sir Barnabas Scudamore could bask in his successful defence of Hereford and his new knighthood, but there was one item left by the Scots army that he felt he had to resolve as quickly as possible. This was the occupation of Canon Frome, an outpost of great strategic importance. In the first instance he approached it at the head of a small party of troops on 9 October and, in a letter which contains only the barest of civilities, summoned the garrison under Major Archbold to surrender:

Sir, I am drawn up into this posture as you see, to summon the garrison for His majesty's service, the which if you shall surrender you shall have termes faire and honourable. If not, I shall endeavour to gaine it by those hands who shall give you and yours the like quarter which they received who lately lost it.
            Sir, I am, your Servant,
October 9th, 1645   B SCUDAMORE
    Send me yr answer in halfe an hour.

In the face of such a letter there was only one reply:

Sir, I wonder you will presume to summon this garrison with so poore a party, I see and know you have with you. I am confident you come hither but for a little contribution which I understand you much want, in collection of which if you will not be nimble I shall send you back in some haste to Hereford, and endeavour to bestow that quarter on you which so forwardly you intimated in your letter.

I am, Sir, your Servant,

October 9, 1645   ARCHBOLD

With neither the troops nor the facilities for a long drawn out siege, Scudamore retired to Hereford to reconsider the problem. In the city at that time was John Abel, a skilful carpenter who may have assisted in the construction of the Town Hall that then stood in the middle of High Town. During the siege he was credited with constructing a mechanical contrivance for grinding corn as well as other works and had been appointed 'one of His Majesty's Carpenters.' Scudamore took the problem to him and the result was the construction of an engine of war that would not have been out of place in the Roman period. It attracted much interest as can be seen from the description in one of the journals of the day: 'The engine was such an one as the like hath not been known since these wars. The Roysterers call it a "Sow". It was carried upon great wheels to be drawn by oxen. It was made with rooms or lofts, one over another, musquet proof, and very strong, out of which were holes to play and shoot out. It was so high that it was above all the works at Canon Froome, so that they could discharge over the works; besides which, a door opened to bring them into the works, out of which a bridge could be drawn for their entrance. The garrison was then in such a condition that had they not been disappointed in all probability this engine had effected their intended designe.'

With this contrivance and about 400 men, Scudamore left Hereford for Canon Frome on Wednesday 5 November. The 'sow' was left with a few troops to guard it about a mile and a half from Canon Frome whilst Scudamore arranged for reinforcements from Worcester. Apparently whilst this was happening, some of the Hereford troops went into Ledbury for refreshments. Inevitably some parliamentarian troops arrived and there was a skirmish with two or three killed and five prisoners taken. Meanwhile, Archbold, having been advised of the 'machine', sent out troops from Canon Frome. They put most of those guarding the 'sow' to flight and brought it back to the garrison. It all seems to have been a very badly-arranged affair and may well be partly due to over-confidence from the Hereford troops following their successes against the Scots army.

With the departure of that army at the beginning of September, Hereford gradually became a refuge for the sick, the disabled, and those made destitute by the war. Included amongst them were some who had been of note, but were no great advantage to the city. Such people as Sir Henry Spiller; Lord Brudenell, a long time sufferer from dropsy; Judge Jenkins, who had, when in office, condemned Parliamentarians as rebels and traitors; and Sir Thomas Lunsford, who had recently commanded, and lost, the town of Monmouth.

Apart from looking after these supporters of the Royalist cause, there were many problems for Scudamore to deal with. One such was an imminent duel between two of the Cavaliers. This had arisen as a result of Sir Nicholas Throckmorton telling Sir Thomas Lunsford 'that he lost Monmouth basely. Sir Thomas told him he lyed: to fight they prepared, but stopt by the guards. 'Twas refered to six gentlemen, but could not end it; they were both confined.' The main problem was the new-found leisure that the garrison had once the siege was over. They had become discontented and quarrelsome and gave considerable trouble to their commander. It was at about this time that Barnabas Scudamore gave such offence to two of his subordinate officers, Captains Alderne and Howarth, that they resigned their commissions and withdrew from the city.

Scudamore attempted to keep his troops as active as possible and at the end of November he took Abergavenny, which had been left with only a few troops in the hands of Colonel Hopton as Governor. They carried off five of the chief citizens as hostages for contributions, but could not spare enough troops to keep the town permanently. These men—the 'roysterers from Hereford' as they were called—also burnt Eardisley Castle, the home of Sir Humphrey Baskerville, and other buildings in the area, and were reputed to have taken part in scenes of plunder at Ross market.

Other scores near Ross were also settled. Wilton Castle, whose ruins are still apparent close to the bridge of that name, is below Ross and on the opposite bank of the Wye. At the time of the Civil War it was the home of Sir John Bridges the son of Sir Giles Bridges, 2nd Baron Chandos, and Mary, the eldest daughter of Sir James Scudamore of Holme Lacy and sister of Sir Barnabas Scudamore, Governor of Hereford.

Sir John Bridges had apparently decided to take no part in the Civil War and instead had sought military service in Ireland. He eventually returned to England to recruit for the losses in his regiment and expressed his unwillingness to allow his house to be occupied as a royal garrison. This annoyed Barnabas Scudamore and Henry Lingen and the resultant action is vividly described by Silas Taylor, a well-known Parliamentarian.

> Near to the bridge of Rosse foreine [meaning outside the town] stood a very fayre sweet dwelling house of Sir John Bridges, which in ancient times was a castle, of which were held several knight's fees in this county; which now being upon mencion I shall make bold to insert something in the defence of this knight, whom the cavaliers unjustly slander with the brand of treachery. He was one yt meddled not with the royall quarrell at such time when Herefordshire was overflowne with that deluge, but it being a time wherein most gentlemen interested themselves on one side or another, he, beeing unwilling to take his rest on his bed of ease while England and Ireland were in flames, betook himself to quarrell in Ireland, as not well understanding the difference in England. At his return out of Ireland, his designe was recruits for his command there, and staying awhile at his house, he found himself in great odium with those that by the late undeserving king were as undeservedly trusted with the command of ye country, viz. Henry Lingen of Sutton Esq: and one Baraby Scudamore, a man of noe fortune, intrusted with ye government of ye city of Hereford, who betwixt them ordered the burning of this house, formerly ye castle of Wilton, which savoured more of spleen and malice than of souldierlike designe, in regard ye place was very unlikely to have made a garrison (it being seated not in a castle-like but house-like building) unless they would have been at ye cost and paines to pull downe the house and built it a castle; but, however, burned it they would and did.

Tradition has it that a body of soldiers set the house on fire on a Sunday morning, whilst the family was at church. This ill-thought-out action led to Sir John Bridges seeking refuge in Gloucester where he became a firm supporter of the parliamentarian cause and helped plan the final attack on Hereford. Thus, the flames that consumed Wilton Castle provided the kindling that was to lead to the seizure of Hereford for Parliament by Bridges, Birch and Morgan and thus, in part, to the eventual downfall of the Royalist cause.

CHAPTER NINE

'A New Tricke to take Townes'

In Sir John Bridges, Barnabas Scudamore had made a doughty enemy. He was determined to avenge his loss and when he arrived in Gloucester he began to explore the possibilities. Colonel Sir Thomas Morgan had recently been made governor of Gloucester and the two men soon established contact and realised that they had the same ambition—to take Hereford from the Royalists.

The young Thomas Morgan, according to several writers, had been a native of Monmouthshire, apparently of mean extraction, who, at the age of 16, was sent to the Low Countries with a letter of introduction to an officer. The officer was not impressed and, so the story goes, said, 'What, has my cousin recommended a rattoon [raccoon?] to me?' The young Morgan was not prepared to take this and left to seek his own fortune, ending up in the service of the Duke of Saxe-Weimar as a soldier of fortune.

Although this is a rather charming story and may have a substratum of truth, Thomas Morgan was actually brought up in Herefordshire, being a member of a local family that moved to Chanstone Court at Vowchurch in the Golden Valley from Llangattock, during the first half of the 17th century. He probably became a regular soldier who, like many others, returned to England during the early part of the Civil War, emerging as a Major in the parliamentarian army in March, 1644. At the siege of Latham House he was described as 'a hot-headed Welshman, with a sharp imperative manner', and was promoted to Colonel. His ability to command must have been recognised, for he was chosen to replace Massey as governor of Gloucester in the autumn of 1645, after Massey had been disgraced by being beaten out of Ledbury by Prince Rupert. Based at Gloucester, Morgan had also been entrusted with the command of the parliamentary interest in Herefordshire. He was apparently a very small man, well known for 'blowing tobacco', and was a victim of attacks of gout. Although he remained a regular officer long after the Civil War ended, taking part in campaigns in Ireland, Scotland and Flanders, he continued to have an interest in Herefordshire, purchasing Kinnersley Castle in 1660. As General Thomas Morgan, he helped General Monk with the restoration of Charles II, in recognition of which he was made a baronet and given the Governorship of the Island of Jersey in 1665. He died in 1679.

As governor of Gloucester, Morgan had no direct orders to attack Hereford, but a third protagonist was about to enter the picture. This was Colonel Birch, the governor of Bath and Bristol.

John Birch was the eldest son of Samuel Birch of Ardwick in Lancashire. He was born on 7 September, 1615, into what was a very Puritan family. In 1633, at the age of eighteen, he moved to Bristol with his brother, Samuel. At that time he was described as a 'pack-horse driver', presumably a trader in charge of his own goods delivering up the Severn valley from the docks at Bristol. Shortly afterwards he married Alice, daughter of Thomas Dean and widow of Thomas Selfe (both of Bristol).

At the start of the Civil War, Birch's commercial enterprise fell into decline with some of his goods being impounded. Like many others in a similar situation, he had little choice but to take up arms and eventually found himself in charge of a regiment under General Sir William Waller. He was seriously wounded at the siege of Arundel in December, 1643, but was taken to London where he rapidly recovered. He then took part in the battle of Cheriton, the siege of Winchester, and the action at Cropredy Bridge in the spring of 1644.

After that action, his regiment was entrusted with garrison duties at Plymouth for some nine months before being transferred, in July, 1645, to help the New Model Army in the siege of Bridgwater. Bridgwater eventually fell and Birch was made Governor first there, and then shortly afterwards at Bath. In September, 1645, a successful attack on Bristol resulted in Birch becoming Governor of that city.

Two other people had an active interest in overpowering the Royalist forces in Hereford. These were the two discontented captains, Alderne and Howarth, who had relinquished their commissions and left the city a little while earlier. They let it be known that they were prepared to sell whatever information they had about the defences of Hereford to the parliamentarian forces.

The immediate events that led up to the taking of Hereford are rather ambiguous as each of the protagonists produced a somewhat different story. According to a paper produced by the Committee of both Kingdoms and published in the Journal of the House of Lords, the leading light was Sir John Bridges:

> That it be reported to both Houses, That, the 11th of November last (1645), upon a proposition made by Sir John Bridges to this Committee concerning the reducing of Hereford, power was given to him, the said Sir John Bridges, to treat with such persons as he should think fit for that purpose, and to promise a sum of money, not exceeding three thousand pounds: That, the 5th of December following, order was given to Colonel Birch, to march with some forces to attend that service, and letters also written to Colonel Morgan, and Sir John Bridges, to give them notice thereof, wherein there was again power given to them, to promise a sum of money to such as should be instrumental in that work, not exceeding, as before, three thousand pounds.

This was more or less repeated in the introduction to a pamphlet published at the time under the title *A New Tricke to take Townes*. The author acknowledged at the time that: 'The particulars of Hereford's affaires with some obscurity hath past the Presse, but for the generall satisfaction of the whole Kingdome (being an instrument in the designe) I have presumed to enter upon a large discovery.' He then went on to relate how:

> Sir John Brydges in his affections most reall to his Countrey, after his continuance a while at Gloucester he came to London, where with the honourable Committee of both Kingdoms, he undertooke with his best endeavours the reducing of the City of Hereford, and the introducing of the Parliament's forces into that Garrison, being cherished by their Honours to proceed in the attempt he returned to Gloucester; from thence disguised he travel'd into some private parts of Herefordshire, and sent to Capt. Alderne, and Capt. Howorth who upon his first summons repaired to him ...

Roe, who was secretary to Colonel John Birch, and wrote his *Military Memoirs*, tended to overpraise his master's actions and as a result gave him more prominence than his actions may have warranted. He wrote:

Returneing to your government at Bath, and Bristoll alsoe being under your charge, you begun againe quickly to bee weary of being out of imployment. Whereupon you went up to London, November the 10th, 1645, and adrest your selfe to your friends there, either to put you in some more active place, or to give you leave to lay downe. Whereupon it was considered by the Committee of both Kingdomes, and they appointed you to drawe out 1,000 foote and your horse, the 5th of December, and to march to Herefordshire; and to endeavour with that force and some from Worcestershire and others belonging to Collonel Morgan, Governor of Gloucester, whoe were to joine with you, in all about 1,800 horse and foote, to endeavour to distress the cittie of Hereford, and use all meanes to take it in; giveing you in hand one weeks pay for your horse and foote, and promiseing you a months pay more if you were succesfull.

According to the pamphlet, it was Captains Alderne and Howarth who, when they met Sir John Bridges, suggested the method by which Hereford could be taken. On his return to Gloucester, Bridges contacted the Committee of both Kingdoms who only then instructed Colonel Birch to help. At the secret meeting:

Sir John Bridges delivered himselfe and desired their severall opinions, so that after an oath of performance and secresie past betwixt them, they concluded that for these reasons the designe was feazable.

First, the conveniancy and scituation of Ailstons Hill which faced the draw-bridge where an army might lie in ambush, yet undiscovered by the Sentinells.

Secondly, the usuall neglect of the Guard and the common custome in not sending out Scouts to Lug-bridge.

Thirdly, the walls of the Priory within Carbine shot of the Gate, being then standing gave an advantage there to lodge the Forlorne party of Fire-locks.

Fourthly, the constant Intelligence Captain Alderne had from the Citie, the which might have prevented any danger, if the busines had eyther been suspected or betrayed.

Fifthly, the contrivall of sending in an Officer with 6 men in the habit of a Constable and his Parishoners. Captain Alderne drawing a Warrent and subscribing the Constables hand of his owne Parish as a returne thereunto.

Sixthly, the assurance of a Reformado Officer in the Citie who was to be neere the Guard at the time of entry, and to hinder the drawing up of the Bridge, as also to be readie to repaire to us if he found any preparation against us.

After the disputeing of these reasons Sir John departed back to Gloucester, with a resolution to Post his man to London for orders from the Honourable Committee of both Kingdomes. Captaine Howorth and Captaine Alderne desired a speedy expedition, and thus determined to dispose severally of themselves. Captaine Howorth was to converse with the Officers in the Citie, and being acquainted with their designes to give upon all occasions intimation to Captaine Alderne in the Country from whom Sir John was to receive instructions, so accordingly to persevere therein. The Committee of both Kingdomes, for the perfecting of this project, finding by these Gentlemens particular ingagements, there was some possibility in the effect, their Honours sent for Colonel Birch, whose regiments was commanded to draw into Gloucestershire, there in readyness to attend the event.

Roe takes up the story when, according to him, Colonel Birch had returned to Bristol from London and was making ready to march to Gloucester. It may be that neither Birch nor Roe were conversant with the plan for they obviously had little hope of success:

Hereupon you went on that hopeless designe; marcht of from Bath and Bristoll the 6th of December, which day it pleased God to begin a great frost, without which it had bin impossible to have marcht at that time of the yeare in those countries of Gloucester and Herefordshire. Comeing to Gloucester you were to conferr with Collonel Morgan, Sir John Bridges, and Mr. Hodges [the member for Gloucester], whoe were to assist you, and advise you howe things stood at Hereford: unto whom when you came, your incouragement was soe small that their earnest desire was that you would march backe to your garisons, it being vaine to thinke of attempting Hereford.

Whereupon you desired they would give your men 3 or 4 days quarters where they now lay nere Gloucester; and dureing that time you would goe into Herefordshire in a disguise, and see if there could bee any hopes of Hereford, or Matchfeild; you then saying that being you were marcht soe farr in soe cold a time, you would beat or bee beaten before you returne. Upon this they were content to allowe your men quarters for 3 or 4 days. Whereupon your selfe, with Sir John Bridges, whoe in that busines was both very helpfull and serviceable, went along with you, both private, first to Ledbury, after to a country house, one Sissels[1], nere thereunto, and from thence sent privately to twoe officers of the King's, whoe upon some discontent had lately laid downe their command, and then were greatly enraged against the governor; supposeing, as indeed it prooved, that those men to bee revenged would give their best assistance and advise.

Roe wrote off the contribution of Sir John Bridges to the plans in a single line, possibly because of his absence from that meeting, but more likely to give additional praise to his master. It is apparent that he did not have the names of the two officers that Colonel Birch and Sir John Bridges met near Ledbury, suggesting that he was not privy to these negotiations. The meeting may well have been at or near Canon Frome, which was still a parliamentary garrison. However, Roe must have been informed in some detail of the results of this meeting for he recorded:

> The next night those men came from there house, 2 miles from Hereford, where they recided, at Nunington[2], and upon discourse with them, it was by you quickly found that they earnestly longed to bee revenged; and you promised them that, if they would assist, and the designe should take, you would give them £100 a peece; and soe enquired what possibillitie there was of a surprize; how there gaurds were kept? whither there were any houses nere any of their gates? what carriages used comonly to goe into the cittie? and if there were any hollowe ground where a bodie of men could lye nere the gate? and what number was in the garison?
>
> To which the reply was: the number of men in armes in the garison, of horse and foote, was about 1,500; that their guards by night were strict kept untill the gates were open; but after the towne mayor was gone the souldiers went to gett their

---

1 Webb wonders if this is Cissells or Cirels
2 Nunington in Withington parish was leased by the Coningsby family during the 16th and 17th centuries

morneings draught, and many times left not above tenn on the guard; that the officers in the towne usually dranke and gamed all night, and lay in bedd the fore part of the next day; that there was within less than musket shott of the gate an ould building called the Priory, where 500 men might lye close; that every morneing sundry carts came in loaden with wood and strawe; and that at this time, the frost still very strong, the governor sent out warrants to the constables in the country to send him soe many men every morneing to break the ice on the mote and river; and that there was a hollow ground behinde the Priory on the other side a smale hill neere the city and about two musket shott from the Priory, where 1,000 men might bee drawne into batalia.

Upon this discourse and further findeing most of their horse weare at that time within the walls by night, you begun to bee confident the towne would easily bee surprised; and your way was, 6 carts; 4 with wood, and 2 with strawe, which were to bee laden hollowe, that in the bodie of every cart 6 men might lye with swords and pistolls; and when they came just within the gate, there being only a bundle of strawe in the hinder end of the cart, they were to through that out, and presently fall on the guard; and that you would lay firelocks in that ould priory in the night to second those in the carts, when the gate should bee open, and they have possession; which would assuredly bee done without suspicion. Thus that designe layd, it pleased God, that hee might the more bee seen, to send that night soe great a snowe that carts could not travell; therefore there must bee a new project; which you instantly thought upon to bee this. The governor, as before, every day sent out men unto the country to breake the ice, the ffrost houlding strong. Whereupon you resolved to provide a man to goe to the towne pretending to bee a cunstable, and to carrie sixe men with him, with spades and pickaxes, great breeches and country habbitt, and a warrant you writt to carry in his hand to avoid suspicion when hee came neere the gate, and a hedg bill under his arme, a usuall thing for constables to carry in their hand.

According to Roe, John Birch managed to find a suitable man to act as constable at Canon Frome:

You went presently to Cannon froom, then a garison for the Parliament, where were many stout fforest men; out of whome for their habit and countenance sake, being soe like labouring men, you resolved to choose your constable and his men. And at last you found one Berow, whose face and bodie promised, when fitly clad, to bee noe other but a constable; and upon conference with him found his resolution answereable and yet his understanding not so pearceing as to afright him with the enterprise: and withall sixe men there fitt for your turne.

There and then it was decided that the attack on Hereford would take place on 16 December and a message was dispatched to the rebel officer in the city to ensure that he would be near the gate at the appropriate time. Leaving Canon Frome, Birch and Bridges returned to Gloucester to inform Morgan that all was arranged and the attack would go ahead.

Roe went into great detail about the methods Colonel Birch used to confuse the opposition. It is certain that on the Monday, 15 December, the army marched towards Hereford but eventually turned back to Ledbury. Whether this was because 'the Foot, by reason of the deepnesse of the Snow, grewe weake and were unable to march further, the Horse though willing were not able to accomplish the busines,' as indicated in the newssheet, or, as Roe had it, part of Birch's 'greate designe', remains uncertain.

Roe takes up the story when Birch returned to Gloucester:

Whereupon you hasted backe to Gloucester, the third day after your departure, and came to Collonel Morgan, telling him you were resolved on a designe into Herefordshire: which hee was soe willing to imbrace that though hee was then sicke of an ague, yet hee would march with you, though under great distemper, which hee did the day followeing [Monday, 15 December] to Ledbury, and all night afterwards towards Heriford in the deep snowe, where some [three or four] of your men ended their dayes in the extremity of the ffrost and snowe. You thus marching on slowly, your designe being not to doe your busines that night, but only to make the enimy the more secure by your returne, day broke when you were foure miles short of Heriford. Whereupon you gave it out to your officers, after they weare all called together, not one of them knowing any thing of that designe, that you would now lett them knowe your intentions, which were these: Sir William Brierton then blockt up Chester; Sir Jacob Ashley and Sir William Vaughun were gon towards him; and you were commanded speedily to march to their reliefe: and you hoped all your officers would beare you witness that the extremity of the wether was such you could not march, and therefore hoped you should well answere it if you went backe to your garisons; to which they all agreed, and the souldiers gladly accepted; and then presently you gave order the souldiers should get some meate and drinke at the next villages, on purpose to give out what you had said of your march thither; only one body of horse to stand ready if the enimy should have marcht out of Heriford.

And the greate designe alsoe tooke well: for the country people desirous to knowe whither the souldiers were goeing, they were as ready to tell the whole matter: and the governor of Hereford not wanting freinds in the country presently was advised of the whole busines. Yet hee for more sureness that day sent out horse, whoe found it true; and that the forces were indeed marching backe towards Ledbury and so towards Glocester: which designe did worke soe that the garison of Heriford was exceeding secure. And yett to make them the more secure, you findeing out whoe gave the governor usuall notice from Ledbury, chose to quarter your selfe at his house; and theire called some of the towne togeather, informeing them of your hard march, and desireing they would give your men good quarters that night, and you would bee gon next day; for the wether was soe bad you could not march as you intended. This they willingly agreed unto; and quickly the governor of Hereford had notice from his freind at Ledbury.

The day past; and it now beeing about 9 of the clocke at night the 16th of December 1645, all having well supped, you called hastily to one of your officers, and caused him to beat up an alarum; which imediatly hee did; and from him tooke all the rest of the drumers: which made not only your owne officers, but some of the townsmen hastily to run to your lodgeing. Where pressing to knowe the matter, you told them that you had advise the governor of Hereford and some others joyned with him were marching towards you; and desired to advise with the officers to knowe whether wee should stay there untill hee came, or rather to goe and meet him, if happily wee might finde them in a hasty disorderly march, and soe breake their bodies.

They, willing to concur with you, said, there was noe way but to goe and meete him, the snowe and moone both giveing light enough.

By this meanes you gott out all your men presently without suspicion either to themselves or the towne, whoe weare charged on payne of death to keepe their houses; whoe else would surely have advised the governor of Hereford. And thus marched you almost to Heriford which was from Ledbury tenn miles [fifteen in modern measure], without speaking one word, still expecting to be engaged; which thoughts kept the souldiers warme that terrible night of frost and snowe: which had it been any other way, you could never have compassed your designe. When you had marched soe far, the officers cam to you wondring they heard of noe enimy; to which you replyed, they are retreated, and if they did thinke it fitt you would march on, with all probabillity before they gott into Hereford you might doe some considerable service on them, they suspecting nothing. Whereupon they every one returned to his place, marching on speedily, but soe silently that a dog scarced barked all the night, though wee marched through three or four villages [probably Tarrington, Stoke Edith and Dormington]; but in deed that was not strange, for if a dog had bin without doores that night hee would have been starved to death. Your selfe in the meane time ridd to Canon ffroom the Parliament garison, sixe [nine in modern measure] miles from Heriford, and there made ready your constable and his sixe men, gave him his warrant, appointed him his bill, and to them their pickaxes and shovells, bound up for them very black rie bread and cheese in course table napkins, soe that to see them goe a man would have ventred his life they had bin country labourers indeed. Thus you went on till you were within a mile of Hereford; at which time the officers againe repaired to you, and heareing of noe eneny, began to say unto you, sure you had some other busines there; to which you did them answere, you had indeed, and if they would keepe close and silent at their charge they should, by and by, see what it was; which they willingly agreed unto.

According to the pamphlet, Captain Alderne took a more prominent position in the impending struggle. He 'kept correspondence with some of his friends in the city' and established that most of the horse had gone to the relief of Chester and 'the Governour himselfe being in some difference with the city,' this was the best opportuntiy 'to compasse a surprize.' The writer states that the troops went from Ledbury to Canon Frome and 'from thence Captaine Alderne with two troopes of Horse secured the three Bridges, vizt. Lug-bridge, Luwarden bridge, and Wordifords bridge[3], by meanes whereof there could no alarm or notice passe unto the Garrison; betwixt the houres of three and foure of the clocke on Thursday morninge the Governour of Gloucester marched up with his horse, the foot seconding him, all rendezvouzd together on this side Aylestons hill; Cap. Howorth and one of Col. Birch's Captains commanded the Fire-locks to the Priory, the counterfeit Constable and his men were disposed to their station; Cap. Alderne shewed Col. Birch the place upon the hill to draw up the forlorne hope of Horse, which was in a large dingle.'

Roe, as must be expected, made Birch more prominent in the action, but he also cast doubts about the reliability of the two turncoat captains:

> Whereupon, being marched neere the cittie, you laid your maine bodie in a hollowe ground which you ffound as you were advised fitt for your turne; thence drew 150 firelocks into that old priory which lay just by the roade leading to Bysters gate. ... and to the firelocks commanded by Leiftennant Collonel Raymond and Capten Browne gave this order, that when the constable was just at the drawbridge they should rush out; and to the maine body, that when they sawe the firelocks run on they should hasten.
>
> Things thus laid, you tooke a speciall care, the officers whoe first you advised with liveing neere Hereford should be soe lookt unto that they should give noe intelligence, which you had reason to ffeare, they expressing some discontent; which caused you to keepe them honerably close for the three dayes your designe was acting, and soe at this present time. Thus the severall parties lay close in the snowe twoe full howers, noe man soe much as stirring, hope keepeing them warme.

The old priory, so conveniently placed outside Bysters Gate, was that dedicated to St. Guthlac. It had been re-established there about 1144 and survived until the Dissolution in 1539. It was bought by John ap Rice who

---

3 The Lugg bridge on the Worcester road; Lugwardine bridge on the Ledbury road; and Mordiford bridge on the back road to Ledbury and the road to Ross

took up residence and was eventually knighted before entering Parliament for Hereford. Around the time of the Civil War it belonged to Anne, the wife of John Seabourne of Sutton, and Grissell, the widow of Arnold Burghill. By that time all of the buildings may well have been in ruins, for in 1675, when the property was sold, it was described merely as 'the site of the late dissolved priory of Guthlac' with no mention of a house. The County Gaol, built on the site at the end of the 18th century, was demolished in 1930, and the bus station and cinema now occupy the area.

The attackers hiding in the ruins of the priory, heard the 'Morning-prayer-bell ring out, and Travalley [reveille] was beaten in the city.' There was even an accidental discharge of one of the raider's muskets which must have sounded loud in the crisp air of the frozen dawn. Eventually eight o'clock arrived and:

At last the gate was opeined; (upon the first letting-downe of the draw-bridge, three men came out of the city, not discerning anybody) and within a quarter of an hower after few souldiers you could see about it; and you supposed, as it proved, that that terrible cold morneing of ffrost and snowe had sent them to a fire. Whereupon you gave notice to the constable, whoe in respect of his cold, which made him and his sixe men goe as if they were almost starved, and alsoe by reason of their broad hatts, great breeches, spades, pickaxes, and bundles of bread and cheese, they might well have deceived a wise man and vigilent comander. Thus went hee on peaceably to the gate; which when hee came close unto, and goeing to shew the officers and souldiers that were with the centry his warrant to bring those men to worke that day, the firelocks rush fourth, and were run almost halfe way before the guard (then busie with the constable) discoverd them. Whereupon the guard began to crye "Arme." The constable with his bill knocks downe one: the rest with their spades and pickaxes fell upon others: this held not one minute, but the firelocks and your selfe fell inn; and presently the remainder of your bodie, with Collonell Morgan; and after halfe an howers dispute in the street, and the loss of about tenn of your men, that great and strong garison, which soe long held out a great army, was taken, and in it abundance of gentry and souldiers; the governor Barronet Scudamore with some ffiftie others escapeing over the river Wye on the ice, which that night was ffrozen soe hard that they were able to goe over.

Bye Street Gate about 1794, copied from a painting by Thomas Hearne

---

The Warrant

Whereas we have received a warrant from the Honorable Governour of Hereford, for the bringing in to the Garrison six able men to worke with such tooles as are fit for your said service, we have in obedience thereunto by our Neighbour Hugh Morris sent a returne of the names of the said parties, viz:

John Baily	Phil. Mason
Wil. Edwards	Ja. Baskerville
Rich. Deeme	Wil. King

These we have sent in by our aforesaid Neighbour, not daring ourselves to appear in respect of the enemies Garrison at Cannon Froome

Dated Decemb. 17	The mark of (J.S.) Jo. Searle
1645	Roger Hill. Const.

Within the city there was confusion as most people were unaware of what was happening. There was some house-to-house fighting which led to several citizens being killed and buildings being plundered. The author of the pamphlet goes into some detail about the fighting within the city.

Whilst they were looking upon it [the warrant] the six men came near with their pick-axes and shovels, and so soon as they were on top of the bridge, the constable killed the sentinel with his hedge bill, and the six labourers killed two more. Then Colonel Hammond, who stood on the hill, gave the signal by holding up his hat to the 150 firelocks that were in the priory, who rushed out and made their way over the bridge, and held it for the horse to enter. Captain Temple led the horse, and first entered, and did special service, for he presently made his way to the main guard, (situated at North side of the castle) where his horse was shot under him, and he fought so stoutly that his sword was broken to the very hilt. One of the troopers was killed, and two others; which was all the loss. The commanders both of horse and foot did excellent service, and came on so gallantly, although they had layne all night in the snow, that they quickly seized all the guard, insomuch that at last many of the enemy passed through the Market-place up to their chambers, and thence discharged their muskets and pistols upon our men (many of the malignant townsfolks did the like out of their windows) which so enraged our men that they slew eight in the streets, but when the enemy saw our men come in great numbers they cried out for quarter. By this means the soldiers fell to plunder and rifle, took what they could catch, from which the governor of Gloucester could by no means restrain them, for they accounted all their own in regard they entered the city by onslaught, and had so much opposition. So every man got what he could, and by twelve of the night they had taken most of the prisoners, only some hid themselves and were not discovered.

As Roe recounted, Scudamore with Lingen and some fifty others, escaped across the frozen river. Following his escape, Scudamore went to Ludlow and then Worcester where he was imprisoned for some nine months for, as governor, he naturally had to shoulder much of the blame for the city's loss. Rather than wait for a possible court martial, he published his defence in advance. This defence was successful in averting the court martial and also provides a somewhat different picture of the circumstances to that of Roe. Scudamore saw Sir John Bridges as the original architect of the plot 'being discontented for the burning of his house.' The following excerpts from the defence have been chosen to illustrate the events and the treachery as seen by someone inside the city:

Upon Wenesday in the afternoone I was advertised that the enemy was marched out of Ledbury, and that the discourse of the common souldier in Ledbury was that they were going towards Hereford. This newes the messenger delivering privately by word of mouth, when Master Major and some halfe a score gentlemen and townesmen were in the roome with me, I did instantly communicate it in publique to them, and directed Master Major to make proclamation, that the townesmen might have notice of this intelligence, and withall be required presently to shovell off the snow from the walls, that the place might be fit for them to stand on with their armes on the first alarum.

About 3 a clock that afternoone, I gave Major Chaplaine orders to double the guards, which he performed not, as by the list he gave me appeares. At 9 a'clock, I dismist the said Chaplaine to go to his rest, telling him I would goe the grand round myselfe, and should expect him to be with me at 5 a'clock in the morning to receive from me the defects of the guards, and to look to the towne while I might catch an houres rest or two, being at 8 a'clock in the morning to sit at a court of warre upon the mutineers of the day before. The grand round I went about one of the clock. ... Going on the round at every port I charged them upon paine of death that neither officer nor souldier should stirre off from their guard; ever adding that the enemie was advancing and the towne in danger. Coming to Byster's gate, at which port they that come from Ledbury enter, I fould the corporall so drunke that he could not give me the word, whom I corrected for the present with my cane, and commanded my Capt. Liuetenant Ballard, who commanded the round with me, to place an officer in commission at that port as soone as the grand round should be ended, and to lay the corporall by the heeles. Looking up I called to the sentinel that stood at the top of that gate to swingle his match, and answer being made that he had a snap-hanz, for the more surety I sent another souldier up and called him downe, and finding it to be so, and fixt and laden, I returned him up to his sentry place, and added one more to him, leaving a strict charge that the sentries should be often visited and relieved every halfe-hour ...

The grand round being ended about 5 of the clock, I ordered my Captaine Liuetenant Ballard to continue rounds without ceasing until 8, and to give me an account ... In place of it, 'tis well knowne by testimony of some who entred the towne with the enemie, that he, the said Ballard, drew off the guard from Byster's gate, where when the towne was entred were but foure souldiers: and further that he had beforehand poysoned, or by some other meanes disabled, the murthering peece which lay in the mouth of Byster's gate ...

The keys received, away he (Lieut. Cooper) hastens ... and passing to Byster's gate, opens not the wicket, sends out no scouts[4], but opens the great gate, lets downe the great chaine, lets fall the drawbridge, and going over himselfe, while he saw upon the other side of the mote the Lieu. and six souldiers who acted the part of the constable and labourers (whose reported pretence of being sent for by warrant Cooper could not but know to be untrue, for hee was the overseer of the works and writ all such warrants and saw the snow upon the ground which made it unfit for work and knew that the ice was every day broken by the garrison) cryes out (and to them certainly) 'Now or never.'

With this the enemy enters: Captaine Howorth being in the forelorne hope of foot that seconded the said personated constable and labourers, Sir John Bridges in the forelorne hope of horse, and Captaine Aldern in the second division. Being entred the gate, where they found but foure souldiers, the fore-lorne hope of horse takes the right hand and seizeth upon the maine-guards, where were but six souldiers and one ensigne; and Captaine Aldern takes the left hand to my house and the castle. My man brings word to my bedside the enemy was entered. I leapt up, commanded him to get me a horse, and slipping on my cloathes I ran instantly downe with my sword and pistoll in my hand to the foregate towards the street, where the enemies horse already come fired upon me, and shot my secretary into the belly: at which I retreating, another of the house shuts the door, and out I got at a back way toward the river, in hopes still of my horse. Upon the left hand at the castle I was shewed the enemy gallopping towards me; upon the right hand going to the Bishop's pallace I found a body of their foot comming into the

---

4 The duty of the Sergeant Major in the morning is described as 'In places of danger he openeth the wicket onely, and sends out some men a pretty distance, to discover whether there be not some Embuscado or the like, and finding all safe, opens the great gate'—Cruso, *Order of Military Watches*, 1642, 65.

pallace yard; and seeing myselfe thus beset, my boy shewing mee that a couple were gotten to the other side of the river over the ice, by which I perceivd it would beare, I passed over, and got to the gate at Wyebridge, where intending to get into the towne at the wicket I saw most of the guard gone, and a body of their horse comming upon the bridge; and then understanding the enemy to be fully possessed of the towne, and no possibility of resistance left, I resolved to cast myself at the King my master's feet ... From hence then I went to Ludlow, and from Ludlow in like manner to Worcester, professing there my purpose to ride to Oxford.

There was obviously treachery afoot in the city during that cold night— treachery at the hands of Lieutenant Ballard, who drew off the guard leaving just four soldiers to their fate, and Lieutenant Cooper, who let down the drawbridge against all instructions and called on the enemy. There is little doubt that these two officers, as well as Captains Alderne and Howarth, were well paid for their services. The Committee of both Kingdoms had, when they heard Sir John Bridges' scheme, promised him £3,000 to treat as he saw fit. The three officers concerned with the attack on Hereford had also promised their help in obtaining the release of friends of Alderne and Howarth and this was also included in the paper submitted to the House of Lords by the Committee in October 1646:

The work being effected, upon report thereof made to the House of Commons, Three thousand pounds was ordered for that service, which was paid, as was appointed, under the hands of Sir John Bridges, Colonel Birch, and Colonel Morgan; That in May following, Colonel Birch signified to the Committee, that there was a promise made, by himself, Sir John Bridges, and Colonel Morgan, unto Major Howorth and Captain Daniell Alderne, two persons that they were to make use of in that service, that, if the work succeeded, they should have, each of them, (besides the money they were to receive) two of their nearest allies such as they should name, freed from delinquency and sequestration, and in June following, Colonel Birch and Colonel Morgan sent to this Committee the original papers containing that promise.

That the said Major Howorth and Daniell Alderne have now desired that Rowland Howorth, Charles Booth, Doctor Edward

Alderne, and James Rodd, senior, should be freed from Delinquency, according to that Agreement.

That the Committee for Sequestrations in Herefordshire, notwithstanding that good service of Sir John Bridges, who was the first instrument that appeared in the county for the reducing thereof, have sequestered his estate, for something done when the county was under the power of the King, and he being now engaged in the service for Ireland, to desire the Houses that his sequestration may be taken off.

And for that it appears there was such a promise made as aforesaid to the said Major Howorth and Captain Alderne, by those who were intrusted with the managing of that business, to offer it to the House to do therein as they shall think fit.

Exr. Gualter Frost, Secretary

Ordered, That this House thinks it fit that the Sequestrations be taken off the Estates of the persons mentioned in this report, according to the agreement, and that the concurrence of the House of Commons to be desired therein.

The rapid capture of Hereford as compared with the unsuccessful six week siege by the Scots army, was received with great enthusiasm in the House of Commons. Colonel Morgan's secretary, who brought the first account to Parliament was immediately voted £30 and Col. Birch's messenger who arrived a little later was granted £20. The 'Constable,' Berrow, received a gratuity of £100 and an annual pension of £50 secured on the estate of Sir Henry Lingen (if it was ever paid) and he became known as the 'Constable of Hereford'.

Hereford's taking was in part due to treachery, in part to good planning based on 'inside knowledge', and in part due to the weather. The method can lay little claim to originality; such stratagems are as old as the Trojan horse. Even so, the capture of Hereford was described as a 'service which had not been paralleled since the beginning of these wars, nor hath the like been achieved for many years in forreigne parts.'

CHAPTER TEN

Hereford and Colonel John Birch

Birch was accepted as the leading light in the capture of Hereford, at least as far as Parliament was concerned. His reputation rose rapidly when the news was proclaimed that a known and tested stronghold had been taken completely by surprise. He was immediately appointed Governor of the city and he received a welcome £6,000 to increase the size of his regiment and pay his men. Roe continued to write Birch's Memoirs throughout the remainder of his military career, which ended with the capture of Goodrich Castle in July 1646.

Although Scudamore and some fifty others escaped across the Wye, there were some 800 people taken prisoner, many of whom were persons of note who were eventually sent to London. Among them were Lord Brudnell, a Romanist who suffered a long incarceration in the Tower but lived to become the first Earl of Cardigan; the Bishop of Hereford and his son; Sir Henry Spiller; Judge Jenkins and Sir Thomas Lunsford. In all there were some '16 knights and manie other persons of quality, with aboundance of Treasure and Rich prize.'

Throughout the day following the taking of Byster's Gate the city was plundered. Some of the inhabitants redeemed their property by paying cash and the captors became possessors of some £40,000 in money and plate, of eleven pieces of ordnance, forty barrels of powder, cart loads of bullets, metal, and ammunition, and various stores including corn and hay.

Birch accounted for the money, setting it against that which was due to him as Governor at Bath and Hereford. It was all included in a formal statement which was passed by a committee of the House of Commons on 15 June, 1647.

The list of payees includes the names of several people who were mayors of Hereford:

David Bowen	Mayor 1641	£20
Richard Philpott Senior	Mayor 1635, 1647	£20
Alderman Evans	Mayor 1629	£27 10s.
Edmund Aston	Mayor 1640	£8
William Cater	Mayor 1645	£20
Thomas Davis (Davies?)	Mayor 1660	£5
Edward Kinge	Mayor 1648	£12
Thomas Church	Mayor 1636	£10
Lawrence	Mayor 1626 or 1661	£6
John Cooper	Mayor 1644	£7 10s.

The ransom money totalled £862 16s. 8d.

The initial pillaging and plundering that took place in the city soon came to an end, but some individual incidents were recorded at a later date. In one case, a man by the name of Philip George was tortured by Birch's men. He was burnt on his hands and feet to try to get him to reveal the secrets of the city. George, an old soldier of the king's army in the defence of Hereford, would not tell. Years later in 1675, a petition to the then mayor, Henry Caldicott, on behalf of Philip George was instrumental in getting him a grant of three pounds out of Harders Charity.

However, following the defeat by the parliamentarian troops, the city rapidly fell into a desperate state—the streets were foul with dung, there were filthy beggars everywhere, law and order had more or less completely broken down, and throughout the city and county the roads and bridges were all in urgent need of repair. John Birch made a start towards resolving the problems by declaring martial law on 15 January 1646.

In some ways the cathedral, as the principal religious establishment in the city; the various residences associated with it, and the Bishop's Palace, suffered even more than the rest of the city, for their problems were to continue.

It was during the Royalist occupation of the city that the dean died and Herbert Croft was appointed in his place. When the city was captured by the parliamentarians, he ran a considerable risk of imprisonment or worse because of his outspoken denunciations of the troops and their ways. 'For soon after the taking of Hereford this excellent Doctor, preaching at the cathedral there, inveighed boldly and sharply against sacrilege; at which some of the officers then present (so little doth a guilty conscience need

Roundel on the cathedral's west front depicting Dean Croft and the soldiers

an accuser) began to mutter among themselves, and a guard of musqueteers in the church were preparing their pieces and asked whether they should fire at him; but Colonel Birch the governor prevented them.' In April, 1649, an Act was passed that abolished deans and chapters and allowed their lands to be sold. The low prices that the properties brought could possibly have been by arrangement, but may well have reflected the rather doubtful security of tenure. The estates attached to the deanery brought £1,071 2s. 8d.

The cathedral canons were also removed from their houses around the close, and the 'singing vicars' lost their homes in the College of the Vicars Choral. Even its library was plundered. When the College was sold, it only raised £220. The potential value may have been lessened since the 'homeless poor'—the vagrants and beggars—had been allowed to occupy the building, or because there had been some damage during the recent siege.

The new administration asserted that there was a need to educate the citizens in an approved way, and Sir Richard Harley was instructed to prepare an ordinance, which was passed on 28 March, 1646 'for the Settling and Maintaining of able preaching and Godly Orthodox Ministers, in the City and County of Hereford.' This had an immediate effect, for three of those appointed (with an annual stipend of £150 and lodgings in the deanery) had to preach regularly in the cathedral pulpit. These new preachers displaced the prebendaries who previously had their appropriate Sunday turns. These new and intruded ministers were apparently uniformly disliked throughout the city with one, Richard Delamaine, being described as being 'grossly ignorant and immoral, flattering the governor into securing for him three benefices as well as his preachership in the cathedral church.'

It was around this time that the memorials in the cathedral church were 'deprived of their brasses by sacrilegious hands'—apparently some 170 brasses were stolen from the monuments, presumably to be melted down.

The Bishop's Palace is located in spacious grounds between the cathedral and the River Wye. Early in the 17th century, well before the beginning of the Civil War, Francis Godwin was bishop. He was a scholar who wrote several books of importance including *A catalogue of the Bishops of England . . with a brief history of their lives.* Bishop Godwin spent much of his time, and eventually died in 1633, at his palace at Whitbourne. Problems followed, for William Juxon and Godfrey Goodman were elected in succession, but for different reasons could not be consecrated. Augustine Lindsell eventually succeeded Godwin but eleven months later he was found dead in his study. In 1634, Matthew Wren was consecrated, but he had only been there for a year when he was translated to Norwich. His replacement, Theophilus Field, died after six months, and George Coke, previously Bishop of Bristol, replaced him. In five years Hereford had had seven different bishops elected and five consecrated.

George Coke, the brother of Sir John Coke, Secretary of State to Charles I, was to stay, but he was a Royalist and suffered for his beliefs throughout the Civil War. He was described as 'a meek, grave, and quiet man, much beloved,' but this had little effect for he was imprisoned in the Tower in 1641, apparently because of his refusal to pay poll money (levied to support the Scots and English armies). He was released at the end of the year on payment of a fine of £60 and returned to his palace at Hereford.

He was again imprisoned following the capture of the city by Birch and was sent, along with other prisoners, to London, but must have been released reasonably rapidly and was allowed to return to Hereford. With the loss of all his official property, even including his private estate at Eardisley, he died a poor man in 1646. He is buried in Eardisley Church where a stone slab in the nave includes his shield-of-arms and bishop's mitre. Following his death, the bishopric remained vacant for fourteen years until Charles II was restored to the throne and Bishop Monk was consecrated. He died at Westminster, without having even seen his diocese, and Dean Croft, the Hereford dean who had stood up to the parliamentarian troops, was elected in his place and governed the diocese with a strict hand for some thirty years.

The bells of All Saints Church continued to be maintained throughout the Civil War, but there are no churchwardens' accounts for the two year period after Birch took Hereford. Some semblance of order must eventually have occurred, even if it was not satisfactory to the populace as a whole, for in 1648 there is the entry:

> Item payd by order from the Committee for wringing
> the 7th of September 1648   6s. 8d.

There is no indication of the quality of this 'wringing', ordered by the hated County Committee, which was presumably to celebrate Cromwell's victory over the few remaining Royalists at Preston on 24 August. The cost of ringing had certainly increased from that paid out four years earlier!

Although the capture of Hereford was a significant tightening of the noose on the remaining Royalist forces, there still remained several pockets of resistance within relatively easy reach of the city. Birch's initial effort was to secure Hereford as a base and ensure that it would not revert to the Royalists again. With this aim in mind, he put a major effort, over a period of some three months, into repairing the castle and making it once again into a stronghold. With a safe and secure base, he was then in a position to release troops for other duties.

Roe describes this period in the life of his master:

> Upon notice of this great worke to the Parliament, they forth-with appointed you Governor of that cittie, which was almost as difficult to keepe as take, lieing surounded with enimies gari-sons; Sir Jacob Ashley at Worcester 20 miles [30 miles in modern measure] of, Sir William Vaughun at Ludlowe with a force; and others at Gutheridge, Ragland and Matchfeild [Goodrich, Raglan and Matchfield]; all the strong garisons lyeing round. Yet God soe enabled you to manage his worke in your hand, that you

kept your horse alwais quartered in the country, (though the enimy dureing all that tyme durst never quarter but in their garisons) and never lost (saving 13 Shropshire horse that came under your protection) one horse to the enimy. And although within the cittie of Hereford was 1,100 townsmen whoe had taken up armes for the King, yet by your speedy ffortifieing the castle you secured that cittie for the Parliament with a few men, soe that though you tooke that place but the 24th day of December, 1645, yet in the beginning of March followeing you had soe strengthened the castle that with the helpe thereof 460 men kept that citty, that the 6th of March you were able to drawe out three hundred horse, and leave a horse gaurd for the cittie; with which 300 horse and 600 foot you then took the ffeild, notwithstanding the enimy all round about.

But in an especiall manner you were molested from Gutheridge with Sir Henry Lingen, whoe had about 90 horse belonging to that garrison . . .

Birch had no intention of living in Hereford Castle himself, the Bishop's Palace being much more to his liking. It was unoccupied and enclosed within reasonably high-walled and spacious grounds. However, the whole complex was too large for his requirements, so Birch bought one half and Captain Silas Taylor the other. At this time the main part of the Bishop's Palace still consisted of the great open hall, 55ft. wide and 100ft long, built by Bishop William de Vere in the latter part of the 12th century. At the southern end, overlooking the river, was a three-storey block over a basement which included some private accommodation. A short distance to the east, and joined to the main hall by a passageway, was another large building containing the bishop's great chamber on the first floor, making it relatively easy to create two houses and yet retain a degree of privacy.

The citizens of Hereford were well aware that there was still a Royalist stronghold only a few miles away at Goodrich Castle with Sir Harry Lingen in charge. Their sympathies would have been with him and they would certainly have had a continuing interest in Birch's attempts to take it. On 9 March, 1646, Birch was successful in burning the stables at Goodrich and taking some 80 horse, but Lingen apparently replaced them with little trouble. A few days later, when Birch had decamped to help the parliamentarian forces at Stow, Lingen decided to make one more daring attempt on Hereford—the type of escapade that is still seen as being typical of the flamboyance of the Royalist forces. At that time Birch had left some 700 foot and 50 horse to garrison Hereford (Roe suggests somewhat fewer), but Lingen arrived at noon, with a mere 30 horsemen. He charged the gate at the southern end of the city, slew four of the guards, cut the turnpike, and would probably have entered had there been any assistance from within. Support was not forthcoming and Sir Henry Lingen returned to Goodrich Castle where he continued to be a thorn in Birch's back for over four months.

Goodrich Castle, in southern Herefordshire, commanded a ford and ferry across the Wye that had been in use since the Roman times if not earlier. This crossing was an integral part of one of the main roads leading into Wales; the historic equivalent of the modern A40. Although designed as a military stronghold, the castle was ill-equipped to survive against the artillery of the 17th century. However, its walls were thick and strong and it would not succumb easily.

On his return from Stow, Birch was determined to remove this irritation, and proceeded to invest Goodrich. The garrison, consisting of Lingen and his supporters, were about to suffer a protracted siege with little or no chance of a reprieve. The offensive started with the use of cannon and attempts at mining underneath the walls. When it had been under way for a little while, Birch wrote a letter to the Speaker of the House of Commons 'from the leaguer in front of the castle' on 18 June, 1646, and said 'I am approached within reach of their stones which they throw abundantly and am now almost ready to play upon them with a mortar piece, which I have cast here; carrying a shell of about two hundredweight; and have planted my battery, and am going on with my mines.'

It was this new mortar piece, possibly cast at Old Forge just up the road from the castle, that eventually became known as Roaring Meg. Described as being little more that a 'toss-pot', it was nevertheless capable of doing a tremendous amount of damage with its $13^{1}/_{4}$ inch shot. Birch recorded six weeks later that 'I had very much torne the Castle with my mortar piece, that no whole rooms was left in it.' Cast on its surface, although now so faint that it can hardly be seen, are the numbers and letters '16 Co. Jo. B. 46.' This can only mean Colonel John Birch, 1646.

Birch's great mine, 'of ten yards through solid rock' under the Ladies' Tower, was opposed by a countermine, but a battery from Roaring Meg so damaged the tower that it fell, blocked the countermine, and opened the interior to the attacking forces. Lingen was forced to surrender and Goodrich Castle fell to the Roundheads on 31 July, 1646, the last of the royal strongholds in Herefordshire to fall. In true Royalist spirit, the

Roaring Meg

defenders are reputed to have marched out to a lively tune called 'Sir Harry Lingen's Fancy'.

After its service at Goodrich, Roaring Meg, then the largest mortar piece in England, was used in the defeat of Raglan Castle and was then brought back to Hereford by Birch. For many years it languished, upside down, as a corner post at the corner of Bridge Street and Gwynne Street until, in 1839, it was moved to the terrace on Castle Green. Early in the 20th century it was placed on top of Hogg's Mount, the north-east corner of the castle defences, where it had two other guns as company. A few years ago it was moved to its present home at Churchill Gardens Museum.

A couple of days before Birch finally took Goodrich Castle, he received a letter from Miles Hill in Hereford which gave him cause for concern. Hill wrote that 'Here it is given out by some, That as soon as Gotheridge Castle is reduced, you are to march away from this City, and another Colonell to possesse your place: And truly I think the design is working: wherfore, if you may use all the meanes you can to prevent it, that your

Brother, or some other friends may command the Castle and Forces which shall be left here, if you do not your self.' There was enough in this letter to cause concern and, as soon as the prisoners had been dispatched to Hereford, Birch followed them and contacted Edward Page, who was the nominal owner of Hereford Castle, having bought it well before the war started. By the end of the day a deal had been struck and Colonel Birch was the legal owner of the castle, which he had restored some months earlier, and all that it contained. It was at about this time that he had to borrow £100, possibly on this account.

Sir Henry Lingen was kept prisoner in Hereford Castle, but after two months he agreed to compound for his estates and was granted his release on 1 October on a promise not to carry arms. Although Lingen had left Hereford, it is evident that Birch anticipated his ability to cause trouble and felt he might choose the day of the great cattle fair in Hereford, 19 October. In an attempt to forestall this problem, Birch called a meeting on 6 October at the New Inn, St. Owen's Cross, to register all Cavaliers in Wormelow Hundred. He had hoped to overawe some of Lingen's supporters—what he did not anticipate was the uproar he found in Hereford on his return later in the day. The details are in a report of the Hereford Committee and indicate how fragile was the peace in the city:

Lieutenant Colonel Lingon, a great Cavalier and very lately in Arms against the Parl. met the Town Major of the Garrison of Hereford in the street, wearing (contrary to his Parole or order from the Governor) his Sword and there after some peremptory or high language given to the Town Major, calling him a Rogue &c: So that a Company of People were gotten together, he openly with abundance of insolence challenged him: But the Town Major perceiving the flocking together of the inhabitants (whose malignity to the Parliament and affection to him and his Family are very well known), feared some Plot of the said Lingon with the Townsmen against the said Garrison—and that this occasion was taken of making an Uproar, to set on foot this design, The rather because at that time most of the Garrison having no Subsistence in the City were drawn into the Country, And remembering that the aforesaid Lingon when he was in Arms against us he attempted with thirty horse to enter the Town at high Noon, when we had at least 700 foot and 50 horse in the Town, Charged the guards at the Gate, Slew four of our men, and, had he not been repulsed by the resolution of

Sir Henry Lingen

that Guard had entered, assured that upon his appearance in the Town the Inhabitants would rise to join with him against the Garrison. Whereupon the Town Major immediately repaired to Lieutenant Colonel Raymond then Commander-in-Chief and acquainted the aforesaid Lieutenant-Colonel with those passages, Desiring that he would give speedy order for his apprehending, to prevent any further mischief, which he readily did unto the Captain of the Watch who found him drinking Sack in a Common Inn called the Falcon, with Mr Isaac Bromwich and Mr Herbert Parrett, both of the Committee.—The Captain of the Watch sent up to speak with Mr Lingon and Mr Bromwich. The Captain of the Watch told them his business: Lingon demanded by what order he came, and what he was—The Captain then replied he was Captain of the Watch—But Mr Bromwich told him, he knew no man that had anything to do to take any man a prisoner.'

The Captain of the Watch did not want to argue with a Committee member and went back to Lieut-Col. Raymond for assistance. Armed with a second order in writing he returned to the 'drunken Bout' and again asked Lingen to accompany him. Again Mr. Bromwich would not agree:

But holding him often repeated, "Thou shalt not go, Thou shalt not go"—And with all reproached the Captain of the Watch, with Scurrilous Language calling him: "Busy, troublesome, saucy fellow", but laying violent hands upon him thrust him as if he would have fallen on him. Whereupon the Captain of the Watch wished him to forbear, Or otherwise he had the power to call up his Guards. Mr Bromwich presently replied, "And I have the power to raise the Sheriffs, Constables, Churchwardens, and other Officers of the County to beat you all out of the Country." Nor was this all, But he reviled the Officers of the Garrison, Saying they were "Cowards, for when any occasion is to fight You know all how to run away": Mr Parrett perceiving the Captain of the Watch and the Soldiers with him much discontented, Desired him to bear with Mr Bromwich, for (said he) you may perceive that he hath drunk very hard—But that if he would let the Cavalier alone, he would see him forthcoming: The Captain of the Watch came and repeated all this to the Lieutenant Colonel who admiring these carriages and passages out of Respect to the Committee repaired to them and acquainted them with all these proceedings.—And withal gave the Captain of the Watch special commands to execute his Order.

In the Interim the Governor returned (it being about four of the Clock in the Evening), unto whom the Lieutenant Colonel with divers other Officers went, Who in the relation of these things, was interrupted.

By this time there was 'a great broil and tumult ... between Bromwich, Lingon, and others fighting in the Inn.' Eventually Bromwich agreed to go along with the Watch. Lingen was left free, presumably because it was considered too dangerous to arrest such a popular figure. Bromwich was brought in front of Colonel Birch at a Council of War, and asked to explain his actions. He refused and said that he would only answer to the 'Court of

Parliament', though, as he was leaving the room, he turned and said to the Governor 'As for you, Sir, I shall answer you in any ground of England.' This was considered a direct threat punishable by death, so the charges were written out and Bromwich was sent under guard for trial in London.

It could have been expected that Parliament would support Colonel Birch as their Governor in Hereford, but this was not to be the case. Bromwich was a cousin of Lord Scudamore and had many friends in the County. The case was taken up by Sir Robert Harley who presented a petition from the grand jury of the county that included charges against Colonel Birch. A second petition from some of the Hereford Committee followed and eventually Bromwich was discharged on giving his parole.

Birch's military career was almost at an end and, although he had suffered a serious setback at the hands of the select Committee of the House that discharged Bromwich, he decided to become part of the political world. On 9 December he entered the House of Commons as a Member for Leominster. In January, when he was temporarily in Worcester, he issued orders to the Herefordshire Committee to quarter his soldiers 'on Delinquents (Cavaliers) and Newters (Clubmen)'. This billeting was unpopular with the County as a whole, so Birch rashly agreed that his regiment should be discharged and then sent for service in Ireland. He considered that this would end his military commitments and therefore he could dispose of Hereford Castle and find a better investment for his money. Thus, on 12 April, 1647, he sold it for £600 to a consortium of Sir Robert Harley, Edward Harley, Walter Kyrle, Bennet Hoskyns, Edward Weaver and William Crowther (who were then the County Members) 'for the public use and Defence of the County.'

However, Parliament did not have enough money to pay the troops what they expected, and when Birch went to Hereford to persuade his regiment to go to Ireland they mutinied 'seized upon the Colonel and his brother the Major[1], and (to boot) the castle of Hereford and £2,000 in it, besides clothes, shoes, and other provisions.' They soon freed Colonel Birch, but flatly refused to leave Hereford and were still there the following January. By July, Birch reported to the House 'concerning some distempers and differences that have happened among the forces at Herefford,' but it was not until October, 1648, that the regiment was finally disbanded, having won their battle not to go to Ireland.

As a whole Herefordshire was not involved in the battles of the short-lived Second Civil War in the summer of 1648, although Sir Henry Lingen

---

1 The regiment had several commanders including Major Samuel Birch, Colonel Humphreys and finally Lieut.- Colonel Wroth Rogers.

managed to persuade some 400 men to join his force. They took part in skirmishes in Radnorshire where Lingen was wounded and captured.

Charles was by then a prisoner on the Isle of Wight, and a Remonstrance, laid before Parliament on 20 November, demanded his death. In order to persuade Parliament to carry out this instruction, the army effectively took control of the approaches to the House of Commons on 6 December and only allowed into the House those Members who supported the Remonstrance. Forty-one members, who had already expressed their opposition to any proposal to execute the king, were arrested as they attempted to enter. Amongst these were several well-known people with previous Herefordshire connections including Sir Robert Harley and his son Edward, Sir William Waller, Colonel Massey and Colonel Birch.

Those allowed into the House became known as the Rump Parliament and decided that Charles should be tried for High Treason by a High Court of Justice comprising 135 members. He was convicted by 68 votes to 67 and executed in Whitehall on 30 January, 1649. Most of the dissidents, who had been gradually released during December and January, returned to the country and left the Rump to attempt to put into force the principles of the English Revolution. Cromwell, who had avoided the Remonstrance, now came to the fore. The House of Lords was abolished and the Commonwealth was formed. For ten years Britain was to be a republic.

Colonel Edward Harley, one of the first supporters of the revolution, continued to oppose the various measures pursued by Cromwell. He had been conspicuous throughout the Civil War for supporting the parliamentarian cause, but when he opposed the Protector, he was commanded to surrender himself prisoner at Hereford to the governor, Lieut-Col Wroth Rogers and was given a safe conduct to go to London and from that time, for a period of ten years, he was not allowed to reside in the county.

Colonel Birch was more fortunate and returned to Herefordshire with the intention of settling down to business. He had money to spend and there was property to acquire. His first, and possibly his best and most profitable purchase was Whitbourne Court and Manor, one of the palaces of the Bishop of Hereford. This was a land of orchards and hops—the latter in one year are said to have produced in excess of £700. He continued his acquisitions of episcopal land in February the following year when he purchased the Bishop's Palace[2] and five of his manors adjacent to the city for £2,475 12s. 5d. The manors were Shelwick, Barton, Tupsley, Bishop's Hampton, Bishop's Eaton and Sugwas. Later, between 1652 and 1654, Birch bought other properties that had formerly belonged to the Bishop

---

2 Directly after his capture of Hereford he and Captain Taylor had bought the palace. It had subsequently been sold but was again available.

including several messuages in Hereford, and a further part of Hampton Bishop. At this time he was living at the Homme, near Leominster.

It is obvious that Birch detested Cromwell's military dictatorship and was prepared to embarrass it at any suitable time. In March, 1655, at the Assizes in Hereford, he said publicly that the trouble-makers were not the Cavaliers, but 'a lot of silly Quakers and discontented persons.' Rashly, he said the same to Wroth Rogers, then Governor of Hereford, who wrote to Cromwell saying that 'I feared such speeches were coales cast abroad to kindle divisions among the good people here, and to hinder their uniting against the comon enimy. I thought it my duty for the safety and peace of these partes, and agreeable to your former orders, to secure him; which I have done, and as his sword was taking from him (he refusing to deliver it) said, though my sword is short now, it may be long enough within a while (the sword hanging by his side being a little short sword) and very angrily asked me, whether I had orders to secure him.' Rogers went on to say that 'I have sent a party to possess his moated house [Whitbourne] (which I finde is very strong with drawbridges, it is alsoe well provided) least at this tyme it might be surprized and manned against your highnesse, and be a great scourge to this country.' Whilst he was languishing in Hereford Gaol, John Birch's manor house at Whitbourne was apparently dismantled.

In 1655, due to the continuing unrest throughout England the whole country was put into administrative districts each under a Major General. Herefordshire was under Major General James Berry. Eventually Berry visited the gaol in Hereford and 'mett with (as a prisoner there) Coll Birch, who hath applied himselfe to me as to a little king, that could redresse every grievance. I confesse upon examination of the busines, though there were some ground of jealousy, yet I cannot see any great reason he should now be kept in restraint. ... I have desired the governour (whose prisoner he is) to give him liberty to be at his owne house upon his promise to appeare when he shal be called for ...' Birch was released in November 1655 having spent some eight months in captivity.

The unrest in the country as a whole was echoed in Hereford where there were many disturbances. A typical example occurred in October, 1656, at the Sun Tavern in High Town. A meeting in an upstairs room included two well-known trouble-makers, John Scudamore of Kentchurch and Nicholas Walwyn of Much Marcle. When other people tried to intrude, a skirmish developed and the constables were called. They were threatened by a Mr. Pitt, who drew his sword, so they called in Wroth Rogers and his soldiers took the rioters into custody in the castle.

Garnstone, Birch's home near Weobley

At the hearing in front of the magistrate, John Norman stated that Walwyn had put down two pieces of gold and said that he would fight the governor or any governor in England. Norman had responded with a piece of silver, but Walwyn threw it disdainfully into the fire. Norman then threatened to throw Walwyn in the fire if he did not fetch it out. Scudamore said on behalf of his friends that Norman had issued the challenge and had struck Walwyn so hard that he fell with his head in the fire. Eventually Walwyn was released on a bond of £40 and two sureties of £20.

Although elected once again as Member for Leominster in September, 1656, Birch was still not allowed to take his seat. He became a Commissioner of Excise arranging the collection of taxes on ale, beer and cider and eventually other household goods. He re-entered the House on 20 January, 1658, but shortly afterwards it was dissolved by Cromwell. However, Cromwell died in September 1658 leaving his son Richard as his successor.

During 1658-9 Birch spoke in the House several times and preserved some sort of relationship with the Rump. The change came with the arrival of General Monck, then leader of the army in Scotland, in London in February, 1660. He gathered together those Members who had been excluded from the Rump including Colonels Birch and Harley. The new 'Convention' Parliament invited Charles II to come and take up the throne. He arrived in England on 25 May, 1660, but the coronation did not take place until 23 April, 1661.

Charles repaid his supporters well and Colonel Birch became Auditor of the Excise for life. The first Parliament of the new reign was elected in January, 1661, when Birch became Member, due to royal patronage, for a seat in a remote part of Cornwall. This Parliament contained many Royalists, including Sir Henry Lingen who was one of the members for Hereford. However, he only attended the first session, for on his way home he died of smallpox in Gloucester and was buried in the parish church next to his home at Stoke Edith.

Birch, having helped in the negotiations for the return of Charles II, hoped to keep most of his purchases of the bishop of Hereford's manors. He secured a promise from the king that he should not suffer 'for severall sums of money by him layd out and for purchasing at second hand six mannors and severall other thinges part of that Bishoprick, and for money expended in building, repairing, and improving the lands of the Bishoprick amounting in the whole to about nine thousand Pounds.'

A similar clause was included in a lease that Birch negotiated with Bishop Monk for some land at Whitbourne. The preamble mentioned the £9,000 and said that it was money spent towards 'the building of a mansion house, together with chapel, stables and outhouses at Whitbourne (formerly burnt down) as well as the Palace at Hereford with six manors ... by order of the King ...' Unfortunately for John Birch, Bishop Monk died and was replaced, late in 1661, by the fervent Royalist, Dr. Herbert Croft. Croft set in motion the machinery for the return of the various properties, but the case dragged on for some ten years until Sir Edward Harley agreed to arbitrate and allowed Birch to retain leases on the properties. In September, 1661, Birch acquired the Garnstone estate as his permanent home. It was close to the pocket borough of Weobley, which still had the privilege of returning two members to Parliament, and as owner of Garnstone he could easily influence the result for all it needed was the support of some fifty burgesses in the run-down borough. His political future was assured and he continued as Member for Weobley from the next election until his death in 1691.

CHAPTER ELEVEN

Damage and Destruction

The areas of the city that suffered most during the Civil War were the suburbs, particularly those areas just outside the gates, and the defences, including the gates, walls and castle. Other buildings suffered from general neglect during the Commonwealth or were deliberately vandalised.

The castle was the most important military position in the city and, according to his secretary, Roe, John Birch spent some eight weeks repairing it and making it secure after his successful seizure of the city. The work must have been reasonably extensive for it included the repair of the tower roof using lead taken from the cathedral's Chapter House. This presumably followed the restoration works at the castle that had previously been carried out by Barnabas Scudamore, but would also have included any repair works needed following the six week siege by the Scots army.

Birch bought the castle in 1646, but sold it again in April 1647 although it continued to be used for the garrison troops. However, as normality was gradually restored throughout the country the number of troops needed to garrison the castle could have been reduced. Whilst the castle remained in use as a base and for the safe keeping of prisoners until about 1660, it was surveyed in 1652 to aid in the eventual disposal of crown possessions by Parliament. Wroth Rogers was then in command having been appointed governor of Hereford Castle by Cromwell. His influence increased when he was appointed president of a commission under which the several estates in the county that had been confiscated were sold to supporters of the Commonwealth at relatively nominal prices. He eventually became a magistrate and was returned as a Member for the county.

A SURVEY
OF THE SCYTE OF THE RUINOUS CASTLE OF HEREFORD, WITH THE RIGHTS, MEMBERS, AND APPURTENANCES THEREOF.

Scituate and being in the Cittye and in the Countie of Hereford, late parcell of the possessions of CHARLES STUART, late King of England, made and taken by us, whose names are hereunto inscribed, by vertue of a Commission granted unto us by the Honourable the Trustees appointed by Act of the Commons assembled in Parliament, for the Sale of ye Honours, Manors, and Lands, heretofore belonging to the late King, Queen, and Prince, under their Hands and Seales.

THE SCITE OF HEREFORD CASTLE

All that Scite of the ruinous Castle of Hereford, with the Appurtenances, scituate and being in the parish of St. John's, and near unto the Colledge and Cittie of Hereford, and adjoining to the River Wye; being surrounded on the West, on the North, and on the East, by a Wett Moate, and on the South by the River Wye; part of which ruinous Castle hath for Inclosure thereof the ruins of an old Wall, with divers Fortifications built upon the said Wall, and without the same; together with a certain Dwelling House now standing in the said Castle, called the Governour's Lodge, consisting of three Roomes below Staires and three above, besides Garretts and necessarye Roomes, with two little Roomes adjoyning to the said House towards the entring into the said Castle; all of which said Scyte within and without the Walls, together with the said Dwelling House and Moate (NB This Moate was partly round ye Castle Green), containing by Estimacion five Acres and a half, more or less, we vallue to be worth per annum £6 10s.

MATERIALS OF THE KEEP

All that Tower scituate in the West part of the Castle, and upon the Mount called the Castle Hill, commonly called the Keep, built with Stone, haveing a Ramper or Wall of Stone, about the same, upon the said Castle Hill, which said Tower is now covered in lead, taken from the Chapiter House belonging to the Cathedrall. All the Materialls of Lead & Stone, with the Timber of the said Keep, wee vallue to be worth, upon the Place, in Gross fortye Pound.

The old ruinous Gate house standing and beeing in the old ruinous Walls on the North side of the said Castle, covered over with part of the said Lead taken from the Chapiter House afforesaid, the Lead and other Materialls of the said ruinous Gate House we vallue to bee worth upon the Place, in Grosse, twentye five Pound.

156

There are two ruinous houses standing and beeing within the said Castle, one of the which said Houses hath been used for the Maine Guard in the said Castle; the other House for quartering of Soldiers in the said Castle, the Materialls of which said Houses wee vallue to be worth upon the Place, in Grosse, twentie Pound.

Memorandum—The said Castle standing upon the River Wye, the possessors thereof, as we are informed, have claimed a privilege of fishing in the said River, and probably have enjoyed the same, but by reason of the discontinuance of Inhabitants in the said Castle, the said Fishing hath of a long time been discontinued, yett we conceave that there is a Right of Fishing belonging to the said Castle, at least soe far as the Bounds thereof doe extend along the said River Wye.

Memorandum—The said castle is now a Garrison under the command of Lieut-Col Rogers; yett because the same was lately given us in Charge, therefore we doe return this survey thereof.

And all Waies, Passages, Liberties, Priviledges, Jurisdictions, Proffits, Commodities, Advantages and Appurtenances whatever to the same belonging, or in any weise appertaining, or which have been heretofore used, occupied, or enjoyed, as part parcel, and Member of the same.

	£	s.	d.
Total value per annum	6	10	0
Gross Value is	85	0	0

This Survey was perfected the 14th December 1652, by us, Viz.
JEREMIE BAINES   JOHN FISKE   SAMUEL COTTMAN

Some two years after the survey of the castle on 2 November, 1654, a Committee, of which Colonel Birch was a member, reported to Cromwell on the possibility of reducing forces and dismantling or demolishing certain garrisons. Regarding Hereford, Birch had stated 'it lay near unto, if not in the very centre of, N. & S. Wales, those mountainous countries, which ... for religion and other things [were] not so well qualified as could be desired. The countries and people there, were not so well affected as he could wish, & therefore this also was fit for further consideration.' Following this report Hereford retained a garrison under Rogers until the Restoration of the monarchy.

The castle was still owned by those who had bought it from Colonel Birch, but they eventually granted it to the Justices of Peace for the County. By 1660, workmen were employed in the demolition of the main buildings and 'a grate part of the stone of the castle was disposed to the

A SURVEY OF A PARCEL OF LAND CALLED
The Barbican, alias the BARGINHAM
LYING AND BEING WITHIN THE LIBERTIES OF THE CITY OF HEREFORD IN THE COUNTY OF HEREFORD

Late parcel of the possessions of CHARLES STUART, late King of England, made and taken by us whose names are hereunto subscribed, by virtue of a Commission granted to us by the Honourable the Trustees appointed by the Act of the Commons assembled in Parliament for such of the Honors, Manors, and Lands heretofore belonging to the late King, Queen, and Prince, under their hands and seals.

THE BARBICAN

All that piece and parcel of ground, with the appurtenances, known by the name of the Barbican, alias the Bargaineham, lying and being within the parish of St. John's, within the liberties of the city of Hereford, in the county of Hereford, and adjoining to the Castle of Hereford, abutted on the east by a certain common washing place, called the Bargaineham; on the south by the river Wye; on the west by a certain orchard commonly called the College Orchard, now belonging unto Lieutenant Colonel Rogers; on the north by the old ruinous wall of the Castle of Hereford aforementioned; containing per estimation forty perches, more or less, which we value to be worth per annum, forty shillings.

Memorandum—That there was a dwelling house upon the said Barbican, but, standing so near the Castle of Hereford, was pulled down in the time of the wars, the residue of which said ground was then a garden and bowling alley, all which was ruined at the same time.

Memorandum—The said parcel of ground, called the Barbican, is said to be holden by one Bryant Newton, by virtue of a lease granted to him by the city of Hereford; but for as much as no evidence was produced to make good the claim of the said Newton, or of the city of Hereford, although summoned thereto, and because the said Barbican was given to us in charge, to be surveyed, as under a rent to the state of the late Charles Stuart, we return the same valued as above.

Signed

JEREMIE BAINES   JOHN FISKE   SAM. COTTMAN

The Barbican must have been the patch of ground between the castle mound and the river, perhaps including the stretch described by Cave a few years earlier as 'ye way under ye Castle, being upon ye same banke, very plaine and open as any highway.' The 'common washing place' was presumably where the arm of the moat, that ran between the mount and the bailey, came down to the river and is where there is still an overgrown access to the river just to the west of Castle Cliffe.

The College of the Vicars' Choral in 1687

College of Hereford [the College of the Vicars' Choral] to build their new dining room, and somme to the city of Hereford to build the Tolsey [a building used for meetings].' The stone had come from the keep and the surrounding wall on top of the mound and once this had been dismantled there was little need for the mound itself. However, it was still present when the Buck brothers produced their panoramic view of Hereford in 1732, and appears partially present on Taylor's 1757 map of the city. Well before this time it had been recorded that 'the gravell of the Castle Mount hath been disposed off by order of sessions.'

All the other buildings in the bailey were dismantled with the exception of the 'Governour's Lodge' and the castle gatehouse. The latter, on the north side of Castle Green, was refurbished and used for a while to store the county records before it too was demolished. By 1682, the governor's lodge had been converted to become a workhouse and for many years it was used as a House of Correction or Bridewell. It still survives as a private house called Castle Cliffe. Within a few years of the clearance works, Castle Green had been landscaped and laid out as a public open space by the curiously named Society of Tempers.

Just to the west of where the castle mound used to stand is the College of the Vicars' Choral. There is no record of the buildings having suffered directly during the Civil War, but afterwards, when the vicars had been expelled, Colonel Birch permitted beggars, who were doubtless very numerous by that time, to occupy the rooms around the cloister. The College was to suffer damage and decay for over ten years and it is not surprising that by the time of the Restoration in 1660 it needed extensive repair.

On the south side of the cloister was the College Hall. At the time of the Civil War this could still have been the medieval great hall of Canon Greene's residence that had become part of the College in 1472. For whatever reason, shortly after the Restoration a decision was taken to demolish the old hall and build a new one. The work was completed by 1676 and Dingley, visiting it a few years later, described it as 'a very fair and square Refectory or Hall looking into their Garden and towards the River Wye.' The present hall is a mid-18th century remodelling and extension of the 17th century building.

The remains of the Chapter House are in the garden area on the south side of the cathedral. It was built in the mid-14th century and was roofed with a fan-vault of an advanced design, probably the work of Thomas of Cambridge and contemporary with the first section of fan-vaulting in the cloisters at Gloucester Cathedral. The fan vault was supported by a central free-standing shafted column and was in a style almost a century in advance of its time. This new building was one of four chapter houses in England which had ten or more sides. It was forty-five feet in diameter and there was a vestibule that joined the main chamber to the cloisters. It had radial buttresses at each of the angles, flanking four-light windows in the sides. Below each window was a wall-arcade of five trefoil-headed arches with carved spandrels. Each of the recessed panels contained a painting. Apart from the outline and foundations, a short section of the recessed panels is all that survives.

The Chapter House did not suffer any damage during the War, but directly afterwards Birch stripped the roof of its lead in order to repair the roofs of the castle gatehouse and tower. This was not an unusual occurrence for the time, but one that should have been rectified as soon as possible after normality was restored. Instead, the building was totally neglected, and at the beginning of the 18th century, the position worsened when Bishop Bisse removed two of the windows and some walling to use in the repair work to the palace. In 1769, the building had become so dangerous that the Dean and Chapter felt that they had no alternative but to arrange for its demolition.

It is fortunate that several descriptions of the building survive including one based on an account of an excursion in the year 1634. One of the visitors provided the following report:

> The Chapter House there is very fayre and not much short of any wee yet saw, wherein are ten fayre square built windows of Antique work in good colours: It is adorn'd on the walls with 46 old Pictures, curiosly drawn and sett out. Christ and his 12 Apostles, the 2 Sisters that gave 4 Mannors to that church. Edward the Confessor and his Queene, The Earl of Pembroke that flourished in the time of the Barrins Warres: St. Winefride, St. Chad and divers holy women. In the midst heerof stands a Pulpitt, wherein every Cannon at his first entrance doth Preach 4 Latine Sermons.

West of the site of the Chapter House is the Bishop's Palace, a building that apparently did not suffer at all during the War, apart from its appropriation and use by Roundhead officers in the period up to the Restoration.

During the governorship of Barnabas Scudamore and the siege by the Scots army, the gates and walls of the city suffered considerable damage. The attack from the south of the river was as fierce as any and the gate that stood on the southern end of Wye Bridge was damaged to the extent that it was useless as a defence for the city. It was abandoned and one arch, the third from the city side, was totally removed and a strong breast work was built behind it. The arch was rebuilt afterwards in a different style to the others, being lower with three stone strengthening ribs underneath.

There is no record of the extent of damage to the other gates and the walls of the city and it may be that the clearance of buildings, orchards and fences around the walled city was sufficient to keep the attackers at bay and save the defences from substantial damage. The defensive works survived for a century and a half after the Civil War, but all the gates were demolished at the end of the 18th century and now only short stretches of the wall and two semi-circular towers survive.

Whilst the cathedral apparently emerged virtually unscathed, the same cannot be said of the city's parish churches. St. Nicholas Church stood at

A drawing of the interior of the Chapter House produced by William Stukeley in 1721 shows how magnificent the building was and how well it had survived since the lead had been stripped from the roof

the top of Bridge Street. At least one authority states that it was partially destroyed during the War and repaired and restored in 1718. Be that as it may, the church was eventually demolished in 1842 to allow the free flow of traffic from King Street into Bridge Street.

The small bridge-head settlement of St. Martin's was contained within an earthwork defence, built long before the Civil War, that had never been improved by the addition of a stone wall. In the face of the Scots army this poorly protected suburb could not be held and the householders would have had to move into the main part of the city and watch their houses suffer under the bombardment of their friends. Just across the bridge over the Wye, on the southern corner of St. Martin's Street and Wye Street, there is an open area that is now used as a car park. Until the Scots army came this was the site of St. Martin's Church. Not long after the siege had begun, a sally was made across Wye Bridge that resulted in the demolition of one side of the church steeple. This was a distinct advantage for the defenders as the higher parts of the church could be used to fire on the bridge and its defences. The church must have suffered considerably for it was totally demolished shortly after the War. It was not until 1845 that the church was replaced on a new site.

The other church to suffer was that of St. Owen. It had been built by Walter de Lacy, just outside the east gate of the Saxon town shortly after 1075. He made use of a triangle of ground between the old, disused defences, the old road that led eastwards from the gate, and the wide new road (now St. Owen's Street) that came from the new town and market-place created by William FitzOsbern a few years earlier. When it was decided to build a defensive rampart, and later a wall, around the new Norman settlement, harsh decisions had to be made to keep the circuit as small as possible whilst including as much of the town as possible. At the eastern end of the town, the new defences had to join up with those that surrounded the royal castle. To have included St. Owen's Church would have involved a large, almost U-shaped extension, almost impossible to defend. Instead the new wall was designed to exclude the church and be as far as possible from it so that the tower would not overlook the defences.

There were several sallies in the St. Owen's area during the siege by the Scots when the defenders succeeded in firing the attackers' works. The Scots, to retaliate, turned their batteries on St. Owen's Church and destroyed it. The church was never rebuilt, but was eventually replaced by St. James' in 1869.

The suburbs of the city—and in particular those areas just outside the gates, suffered at the hands of Barnabas Scudamore, who was determined to ensure that the city could withstand a siege successfully. The wholesale removal of buildings, walls, hedges and trees would have left clear areas of fire for the defenders and made a close approach by the besiegers impossible. The available documentary sources only record the loss of a few buildings, but many others would have been affected, especially the houses of the poor living close to the edge of the city.

Almshouses, or Hospitals as they were usually called, were quite often built well outside the defences, presumably because suitable sites could easily be obtained. One such complex was a little way out along St. Owen's Street where there was the twelfth century round chapel of St. Giles which originally belonged to the Knights' Templar. Adjoining it were two sets of almshouses; one, St. Giles, founded in 1290, and the other provided by a Richard Williams in 1601. The latter foundation, along with many others, was neglected during the War, became ruinous and was rebuilt shortly after the Restoration. A similar reason may well lie behind the rebuilding of St. Giles chapel as a small, almost square building in 1682.

The end of the Civil War led to a series of other losses—those works that had been deliberately built for use during the War and were just as deliberately demolished afterwards so that they could not be used again. They would have included earthwork defences and mines dug by the Scots army on one side of the wall during the siege, and countermines dug by the defenders on the other. Their positions are now lost and are only likely to be rediscovered by accident, such as the mine in the St. Owen's area that was flooded, drowning its miners; defences such as the probable bank and ditch to the east of the city, afterwards levelled out so that no trace remained. And where was the temporary bridge built across the Wye?

The visible traces of the Civil War are slight. There is the Row Ditch embankment across Bishop's Meadow, used in attacks against the castle. Even less apparent is the slight earthwork that joins two parts of the Wye at Bartonsham, forming the landward defence for the Scots leaguer. Then there is the enigmatic Scots Hole, adjoining Old Eign Hill once the main road to Mordiford Bridge. Was it used by the Scots or was it the hiding place for Colonel Birch's main army when he practised his 'new tricke to take towns?' And who fired the cannonball which lodged high up in the city wall close to the site of Friars' Gate?

BIBLIOGRAPHY

GENERAL WORKS

There are many general works on the Civil War. The following are relatively recent and easily accessible:

Downing, T., & Millman, M., 1991, *Civil War*, (Ch. 4 Television), London

Porter, S., 1994, *Destruction in the English Civil War*, Stroud

Sherwood R., 1992, *The Civil War in the Midlands*, 1642-1651, Stroud

LOCAL WORKS & REFERENCES USED IN THE TEXT

Blair, J., 1987, 'The 12th Century Bishop's Palace at Hereford', *Medieval Archaeology*, XXXI

Collins, W., 1915, *Historical Landmarks of Hereford*, Hereford

Duncumb, J., 1804, *Collections towards the History and Antiquities of the County of Hereford*, Vol. 1, Hereford

Heath-Agnew, E., 1977, *Roundhead to Royalist, A Biography of Colonel John Birch*, Hereford

Johnson, R., 1868, *The Ancient Customs of the City of Hereford*, London & Hereford

Lewis, T.T., 1854, *Letters of the Lady Brilliana Harley ...*, Camden Soc., London

Price, J., 1796, *An Historical Account of the City of Hereford ...*, Hereford

Robinson C.J., 1872, *A History of the castles of Herefordshire and their Lords*, Hereford

Robinson, C.J., 1872, *A History of the Manors and Mansions of Herefordshire*

Shoesmith, R., 1980, *A Short History of Hereford Castle*, (pamphlet), Hereford

Smith, L.T., 1964, *The Itinerary of John Leland*, (5 vols.) Illinois, U.S.

Townsend, G.F., 1866, *The Sieges in Herefordshire during the Commonwealth ... A lecture ...,*' (Pamphlet), Leominster etc.

Watkins, A., 1919, 'Roaring Meg,' *Trans. Woolhope Natur. Fld. Club*, (1918-20), 172-74

Watkins, A., 1933, 'Foundations of Buildings in Hereford Castle,' *Trans. Woolhope Natur. Fld. Club*, (1933-35), 36-40

Webb, J., 1857, 'Some Passages in the Life and Character of a Lady resident in Herefordshire and Worcestershire during the Civil War ... collected from her Account-book ...,' *Archæologia*, XXXVII, Society of Antiquaries, London

Webb, J., (ed) Webb T.W., 1873, *Military Memoir of Colonel John Birch ...written by Roe, his Secretary ...*, Camden Soc., New Series, VII, London

Webb, J., (ed) Webb T. W., 1879, *Memorials of the Civil War between King Charles I and the Parliament of England as it affected Herefordshire and the adjacent counties*, 2 Vols, London

Wharton, N., 1853, 'Letter IX' in 'Letters from a Subaltern in the Earl of Essex's Army ...', *Archæologia*, XXXV, 331-33

Whelan, B., 1926, 'Hereford and the Civil War,' *The Dublin Review*, (July-Sept 1926), 44-72

Winnington, T., (ed), 1687, *Dingley's History from Marble*

Also from Logaston Press

Monuments in the Landscape Vol 1
—A Guide to Prehistoric Sites in Herefordshire
by George Children and George Nash. The history, archaeology and anthropology of the county's prehistoric period. With a detailed guide to the major sites, this book helps explain the settlement of Herefordshire and the progression from nomadism to the centralised hilltop settlements of the Iron Age. 144pp £6.95 ISBN 1 873827 09 1

Owain Glyn Dwr
The War of Independence in the Welsh borders
by Geoffrey Hodges, this book concentrates on the background to and the actual fighting in the borders. The tensions leading up to the revolt are considered, as are the politics of early fifteenth century England and Wales. The battle of Pilleth is examined in detail, as is the Franco-Welsh advance on Worcester. Finally the evidence is detailed for Owain spending his last days with his daughters in Herefordshire. 256pp £9.95 ISBN 1 873827 24 5

James Wathen's Herefordshire 1770-1820
A collection of his sketches and paintings
by David Whitehead and Ron Shoesmith. This is a limited edition book of which only a few copies remain. With 90 waterclours and engravings, it depicts and describes the city and county at the time of the picturesque movement. For details and brochure, contact Logaston Press.

The Spirit of Herefordshire
by Jill Howard-Jones. Twenty-two Herefordshire characters tell their own stories, extrapolating from known facts, or occasionally from long-believed folklore. Suitable for young and old alike, with numerous illustrations. 176pp £7.95 ISBN 1 873827 14 8

Walks & More
by Andrew Johnson and Stephen Punter. A walking and guide book covering central Wales, Herefordshire, Worcestershire west of the Severn and southern Shropshire. 80 circular walks, a gazetteer to over 150 towns, villages and places of interest, plus chapters on history, agriculture, folklore, cider, beer, art and literature. 336pp, illustrations, maps. £7.95 ISBN 0 9510242 6 4